Hallelujah Anyhow!
Suffering and the Christian Community of Faith

Diedra Kriewald

Published by
Mission Education and Cultivation Program Department
for
The Women's Division
General Board of Global Ministries
The United Methodist Church

Published in the United States of America
Library of Congress Catalog Card No: 85-81103

Cover art: Graphic Art Design

Please send any comments or critiques about the text to Literature Editor, Room 1356, General Board of Global Ministries. The United Methodist Church, 475 Riverside Drive, New York, N.Y. 10115.

For Inzer
Who Has Stood by Me

CONTENTS

TEACHER'S GUIDE

PREFACE

The Central Theme—Canonical Stories

A "canonical story"[1] is a narrative that is accepted by religious faith as an authoritative account of human experience. While "the canon" is the particular writings accepted by the church as authentic scripture, canonical stories are not authorized by any official church body and do not expound doctrine. They are stories of "the people" and incidents from the lives of real folks, or, we might say, "Christianity from below." A canonical story rings true to our own life experiences. Sallie TeSelle puts it this way:

> Life is tough. That is hardly a novel thought, but it is nevertheless the backbone in a literal sense—the "structure"—of a good story. We recognize our own pilgrimages from here to there in a good story; we feel its movement in our bones and know it is "right." We love stories, then, because our lives are stories and in the attempts of others to move, temporally and painfully, we recognize our own story. For the Christian, the story of Jesus is the story par excellence.[2]

The story of Jesus provides a model of how to interpret our own experiences. The church recites the drama of the people of God found in the Old and New Testaments. The biblical narratives provide a standard for us in that they tell us about the kind of God who stands with us, and they help us to test and judge our own stories.

Hallelujah Anyhow

The church also preserves the faith stories of Christians through the centuries who witness to the power available to

---

[1]The term, "canonical stories," comes from an essay by Stanley Hauerwas and David Burrell in *Truthfulness and Tragedy, Further Investigations Into Christian Ethics* (Notre Dame: University of Notre Dame Press, 1977), chapter 1.

[2]Sallie TeSelle, "The Experience of Coming to Belief," *Theology Today*, July, 1975, p. 159.

each of us during times of tragedy. These witnesses testify that the promises of God are true and that we do not have to cling to destructive alternatives. No matter how miserable we feel, they testify that our suffering can be redeemed.

"Hang on to Jesus!" "Hang on to the promises of God," say the witnesses—even through grief, anxiety, depression, violence, oppression, hunger, and yes, even the possibility of facing martyrdom. There is hope for new life, and they show us by their true stories, how to go on faithfully. Canonical stories ring with the conviction, that in spite of the troubles of life, a victorious Christian will be able to sing, *"Hallelujah, Anyhow!"*[3]

Suffering and Courage

Christians have wrestled with the reasons for suffering over the centuries. The church has never endorsed any one answer to questions of theodicy. "Theodicy" is a term indicating the investigation of why evil exists in a world created by a good God. Questions of theodicy will be raised throughout the book, although no claim is made for any one position. The issue of this spiritual growth study is not so much "why" suffering exists, but rather what resources are available within the Christian community to aid believers in times of catastrophe.

The focus of this book is suffering, but more, it is *courage.* The central theme expresses that the stories of the people of God (ordinary and extraordinary, past and present) help pilot us through the inevitable storms of life. John Shea has suggested that the perennial Christian strategy is to:

1. Gather the folks.

2. Break the bread.

3. Tell the stories.[4]

---

[3]"Hallelujah, Anyhow" is a watchword of The Young and Adult Choir of the Alfred Street Baptist Church in Alexandria, Virginia. "Hallelujah, Anyhow" is the title of an original gospel musical presented for the 26th anniversary service of the Young and Adult Choir.

[4]John Shea, *Stories of God, An Unauthorized Biography* (Chicago: The Thomas More Press, 1978), p. 8.

With one of my students I would add a fourth strategy—

4. Act on the story.[5]

We begin with my own story, or at least one part of my story that deals with suffering and the Christian community of faith. The book starts here, not because my struggle was more interesting or my solutions more profound than those of another but because my history provided the lenses that helped me map a path through suffering. I am able to speak of the larger context of the world inasmuch as I have been forced to grapple with the issues of suffering in my own life. I suspect most of us approach the topic of this book with the help of a very personal framework. I invite you to join with me by exploring your own individual stories in light of the canonical stories of the church.

---

[5]Carla B. Gorrell, ''The Church and Its Ministry,'' A Master of Divinity Senior Project, Wesley Theological Seminary, 3 September 1985, p. 8.

Chapter I

SAN JOSE ITURBI, MEXICO, JULY 1962

Funny, isn't it, what insignificant details are remembered after a major crisis. A small bare light bulb was the only means of illuminating the cavernous entrance to the town hall on the night of the accident. The town hall was at San Jose Iturbi in the country of Mexico. Back somewhere in the labyrinth of rooms and halls were the bodies of my young husband and three youths killed in a car-truck accident.

We had been on a work camp project sponsored by Centenary Methodist Church in Winston-Salem, North Carolina. Working with Mexican youth, we were contributing to the building of a summer camp near Monterrey. Our task finished, the group was headed south on holiday. I remember thinking that night about the great events thus far in my life: I was a college and seminary graduate, had traveled twice to Europe and extensively in the U.S., Canada and Mexico, was married to my first love and happily engaged in ministry. Suddenly, I was twenty-five years old and a widow. Four months later, I wrote a poem about that night and titled it for the name of the town.

San Jose Iturbi

Hell is not fire and
Brimstone, nor Lucifer waiting
to pitch the unwary into a
caldron of burning flesh.

1

Hell is a tiny lightbulb
Vaguely illuminating documents
to be filled out in a huge,
damp room bare but for table,
typewriter and certificates.

Name? Born?
Home Address? Names?
   Questions, Questions, Questions
To be answered in the
fifty-watt dimness.
Shadows are catching the
distorted features of busy officials.
   Waiting, Waiting, Waiting
To identify a dirty bag, full
of blood stained items.

I move outside into the dusk.
Unpaved streets circle the square
with ruts so deep a car seems to be
the antique beside the burros.
The plaza is burdened, burdened,
burdened by an overflow of scrawny
dogs and the human curious. Official
vultures watch me waiting for
peso bribes to release the dead.

Inside me I'm burning, burning,
burning feeling the stares of those
casually scattered around the square;
Eyes gazing passively at the American
girl, who stands alone—
fiercely proud.

The "Brave Witness" Piety:[1] Grief and Anger

Most mourners find some negative ways of handling
tragedy. I took up cigarettes and appreciably increased my
caloric intake. At the time, it seemed to be a fairly innocuous
way for a religious professional to protest this unexpected
fate. My small rebellion did not go unnoticed. Later in the

---

[1]The word "piety" indicates the type of dutiful conduct that is expected
of a religious person.

summer I was seen smoking at a youth conference. I received a letter from a well-intentioned home missionary who suggested that I would be more effective in youth ministry if I did not smoke. All my anger at the injustices of life exploded over that letter. Receiving the letter was one of the few occasions that I allowed what I thought were "negative" emotions consciously to surface. Anger did not come easily to me in those days.[2]

Any negative protest was minor. I had a clear image of how a Christian church worker publicly handles tragedy. Cheerfully continuing to function in ministry, comforting others in greater need, and devotedly spending long hours in service characterized my ongoing lifestyle after the accident. While I put up a brave public front, some lines I wrote at that time indicate the true nature of my grief.

At the Grave

My insides scream
   "I want to be alone!"
Alone to think
to cry
to feel again.
Why must you intrude?

Tears are now impossible.
Yet, I retch
internally, required to
carry on superficialities.

I stare at the ground
muttering answers, cognizant
only of the faded daffodils so
incongruous, vased upon the winter's earth.

My hands are steady, speech
even. Only my stomach betrays
the pain, knotted by
uneasiness and guilt.

---

[2]An excellent chart on the ways people grieve may be found in Mary Ritzman Ebinger, "Alone," *Beginnings and Beyond: A Collection of Playlets for United Methodist Women*. Leaders may wish to discuss the Ebinger material with their groups in connection with this section of the chapter.

I make you cry—that
which I wished for myself.
In the end you won.
I left before being alone.

I had trouble displaying both anger and grief. Somehow I had contracted the notion that a Christian must present a brave witness to the world during adversity. The governing idea that somehow I must be a valiant model for the church actually hindered the healing process.

How liberating was the day, a few years later, while reading Matthew 23:13-39, I suddenly noticed that Jesus was really angry. Naturally, I had read this scripture before, but somehow I had missed the emotion. I decided to read the passage out loud to myself as if I were an increasingly emotional Jesus. Slowly increasing the tempo and the volume of my voice as the passage progressed, to my astonishment I was yelling. Lowering my voice almost to a whisper, I concluded sorrowfully, "How often have I longed to gather your children, as a hen gathers her brood under her wings; but you would not let me." The content of what I was reading was far less important than the freeing emotion of participating vicariously with the anger of Jesus.

I read the Gospels straight through the next day looking for other examples of irritation, anger, sorrow and regret. At the conclusion of this biblical exercise, I realized that the "brave witness" piety was false and had most certainly blocked the natural healing emotions. Severe loss will quite naturally bring out deep and conflicting emotions. When feelings are discounted we close down the healing process. These strong feelings should be accepted and not feared. Healing begins when we listen to the playing of our inner flute.

The flute of interior time is played
whether we hear it or not,
what we mean by "love" is its sound
coming in.
When love hits the farthest edge of excess,
it reaches a wisdom. . .[3]

[3]Kabir, lines from *The Kabir Book*, Trans. Robert Bly (Boston: Beacon Press, 1977), p. 21. Reprinted by permission of Beacon Press.

Theological Framework

The Church (through congregational, college and semi-nary education) provided me with a sound, theological framework with which to understand and cope with the tragedy. In my mind, I was absolutely certain, for example, that God had not personally caused or predestined the deaths of these four Christians. No devils stalked the Mexican highway. And there was no secret sin or fault that moved events, as Job's three friends had tried to suggest. Adamantly rejecting one pastor's suggestion that these deaths were somehow a part of God's larger plan, I did not believe that what had happened so suddenly was the intentional will of God.

For me, as for many other sufferers, Leslie D. Weather-head's small book, *The Will of God*, was one source that provided a religious framework for discerning the mystery of God's role in tragedy. God had created an orderly world, I reasoned, so that it was only God's circumstantial will that death would occur when a vehicle traveling at high speed slammed into a parked truck. The consequences of "natural law" make it inevitable that fragile human bodies will be broken. I had no problem, however, assigning to God the ultimate responsibility for Richard's death, in that the creator of this cosmic system surely knew all the conse-quences of that natural law, both good and bad.

God was not powerless to act against evil; but I certainly did perceive that any understanding of the exercise of that power in the world was beyond my understanding. Intuitively, I sensed that luck and chance, as well as the genes we inherit, play a major role in our destiny. I accepted the latter without reservation and found comfort in the fact that God was not playing favorites within the human race.

Human error and perhaps "sin" was also on the Mexican road that night. Our group was traveling after dark, as we had promised ourselves not to do, and an inexperienced driver was at the wheel. The object of impact was a truck parked on the highway. We never knew for certain why the truck was parked there, although it was rumored that the driver was outside, drunk beside the road. In the years immediately following the accident when I struggled with

5

these realities, John Hick published his now classic book entitled *Evil and the God of Love.* Hick's work was helpful because it allowed me to see where my own thinking about sin and death fit into the several different streams of Christian thought.

John Hick's study led me to identify myself, as I still do, with those theologians who follow a school of Christian thought that has come to be known as the Irenaean school. This typology for explaining sin was first set forth by Irenaeus, who was the Bishop of Lyons around A.D. 200 and who is considered by many to be the author of the church's first systematic theology.[4]

The first line of an essay on suffering by twentieth century theologian Pierre Teilhard de Chardin seems to capture a foundational premise of the Irenaean school of thought. Teilhard writes, "In the first place the world is under construction."[5] If the world were not created perfect but is still under construction, then sin and evil do not emerge from a single historic "fall." In this view, evil cannot be traced back to the common rebellion of two finitely perfect beings named Adam and Eve.

The earth and the human beings who populate the planet are one part of an unfinished creation. The story of Adam and Eve may imply that humanity was created not in some paradisiacal state but in an earthly garden at the beginning of our growth and development in God's continuing providence. Our ancient ancestors were endowed with moral freedom and personal responsibility, just as we are today. Their personal freedom included the capacity for rebellious action and for decision making that might be both self-destructive to themselves and injurious to others. The driver of that parked truck, therefore, was not an evil

---

[4] Irenaeus has been called, "The earliest theological leader of distinction" in the early church. He was born in Asia Minor, brought up in Smyrna, and spent his ministry at Lyons in Gaul, in what is now France. His greatest work, *Against Heresies,* was written in A.D. 185 to counter the Gnostic heresy. It must always be remembered that Irenaeus was a second century Christian. Even though he proposed an original interpretation of its meaning, Irenaeus did believe in a literal fall.

[5] Pierre Teilhard de Chardin, *Human Energy* (New York: Harcourt Brace Jovanovich, 1969), p. 48.

person caught in the damnable rebellion of some remote ancestors who existed at the dawn of humanity. Furthermore, my husband was not a terrible sinner for making an unwise travel decision. Both men were a part of a very complex and unperfected cosmos. The decisions of both men, however, had enormous consequences for themselves and for many others.

The struggle to become sanctified (perfected or holy) is a lifelong process facilitated by God's grace. To affirm that the cosmos is still under construction does not mean a belief in some simple evolutionary formula of moral progress. Indeed, physical pain and mental anguish seem to be distributed at random and often in what appear to be meaningless ways. Some deaths do have dignity and purpose, such as a peaceful end after a long and honorable life. Martyrdom, in the name of a just cause, may justify the grief of survivors, but some deaths are essentially meaningless. I consider the deaths of my husband and three friends to be in that category. All suffering does not have a noble end.

The Irenaean tradition suggested to me that all of us are created into a world of good and evil, of sin and struggle; nevertheless, this is the *only* world that we have, and life in this universe is the arena that has been appointed as the environment for humanity's spiritual development. It was a healthy decision when I finally declared that I would never understand to what end or ultimate purpose this universe was created. I also believe we are better off refusing to rationalize the incidences of suffering with theories that trivialize the harshness of its reality. So I tried not to play "what if" games, that is, "what if we had started earlier in the day," or "what if the other driver had made a side trip to the market for vegetables." The events of 24 July could not be changed. Playing "what if" in times of sorrow is surely a tortuous game.

Recently, I talked with Ruth about the death of her husband. A lifetime of destructive decisions caused severe physical problems for Ray at the end. He smoked heavily and was diagnosed with emphysema. His alcoholic consumption was high and he developed cirrhosis of the liver. He was obese, which aggravated a heart condition.

7

He died from "complications." Ruth kept asking me why Ray died so young. She also wanted to know why God had taken Ray just when he seemed to be recovering. "What if," she cried, "there had been more time for this new treatment."

Deep down Ruth really knew why Ray had died. There was no mystery about his death. Years of self-destructive decisions preceded the actual event. Yet, Ruth persisted in trying to find cosmic purpose in the death of the one she loved. Perhaps the honest truth seemed either too simple or too judgmental of Ray. Ruth's theology seemed to demand God's personal intervention in Ray's case. To be sure, Ray would have died someday, as Ruth herself must also die, for death is the natural end for us all. But, in this case, to recognize that her husband had the principle moral responsibility for his own early destruction was very difficult. Why Ray died may not be a mystery. Perhaps the more haunting question for his survivors and for us is, "why does a rational, competent individual insist on obviously destructive behavior?" This may be the ultimate concern behind Ruth's questions.

While no one religious framework provides all the answers, the theological structures that I had adopted for dealing with sin and death kept me from torturing myself with the kind of questions that plague Ruth. I drew enormous comfort from various biblical images. The theology of the cross, that is, meditation on the sufferings of Jesus, was never very helpful to me, although such an image has been of great comfort to countless Christians. The Christian hope for new life drawn from the images of the resurrection were reassuring to me both about the status of those who had died and in facing my own inner turmoil. Augustine's affirmation, "We are the Easter people," characterized my stance as I steered the slippery intellectual course between an honest recognition of suffering and the hope in the power of God to transform what seemed so bad into something good.

Now more than two decades later, the theological insights that helped me survive the accident of 1962 are among those principles that still guide today, although I have a deepened appreciation for the tenacity of evil.

8

Basically, I had already adopted a position that helped explain the Mexican accident. I am very grateful to my Church for such guidance.

The Panic Attacks

I thought I was handling the tragedy with stoic grace in spite of a persistent and intense sadness. Yet it was bothersome to feel as though somehow my future was gone, that is, the future in which I had invested so many youthful hopes.

Without warning, over a year later, I broke into a cold sweat, my heart began a wild beating and an intensive fear gripped my whole body. It was the first of a series of panic attacks that would last off and on for a full decade. Anxiety broke over me in giant waves, overwhelming and terrifying in their intensity. One year after the first panic, I was having difficulty forcing myself into public occasions where the unwelcomed attacks often began. In addition, I was put in the hospital to monitor an excessively high blood pressure and my thyroid gland picked this moment to slow down its work.

Life was not fair! I reasoned that nothing like this should be happening. After all, I had a family that cared for me, a network of supportive Christian friends to sustain me and the advantage of a working theological framework to handle the difficult religious questions. I was in graduate school studying Christian doctrine. Nothing about this anxiety was logical or reasonable.

Not until later did I become aware of the simple psychological data that would have quite accurately predicted some type of adverse reaction. Religious doctrine does not heal the pain of loss and loneliness. Medical research has proven that a major change of environment soon after the loss of a spouse is likely to produce illness. I had left my primary support community to move 300 miles away to attend graduate school, and I also went from living with a supportive friend to coping by myself in an efficiency apartment on the eleventh floor of the married students' apartment building. One of the things I remember most about that year was the dramatic thunder storms that I watched from the picture window that covered the length

9

of the small apartment. I felt a great kinship with the psalmist who wrote:

> I am like a desert-owl in the wilderness,
>   an owl that lives among ruins.
> Thin and meagre, I wail in solitude,
>   like a bird that flutters on the roof-top. (Psalm 102:6-7, NEB)

As the anxiety worsened, it finally became clear that I wasn't suffering from unresolved childhood experiences. Even though I rejected all notions of any real demons, I did understand why the biblical people might have felt possessed by evil spirits. It just did not seem possible that this unknown and unnamed fear could be coming only from me.

A fancy religious term for what I was experiencing might be called "existential dread," that is, the loss of present meaning and the fear of the future. I no longer trusted the universe to be a friendly place or believed in my own capacity to exercise control over events. The powerful interplay of memory and the anticipation of the future led unconsciously to what I perceived as a loss of control over my life. I must hasten to add that it took many months to understand what was happening. For a long time, there was only the mystery of why Diedra the adventuresome, who had always loved air travel, was now Diedra the fearful one, afraid to board an airplane. The answer to the puzzle was relatively simple. In trying to protect myself from further hurt, my unconscious mind kept warning me about situations in which I was not in control. To fly was to turn my destiny over to unknown pilots.

I also played a very destructive inner game that I called "catastrophe." Panic would be brought on if a significant friend were flying (or traveling anywhere for that matter) or if that friend were inexplicably late. I wrote on one such occasion:

> I stood on the waters.
> Like a child stumbling for
> first steps I held forth my
> hand. My friend's touch provided
> safety enabling me to walk.
>
> Step. . . Step. . . Ste. . . st
> sthe fear dawns—terror of
> losing the hand. While

10

fumbling to help, we pull
each other under and sink
drowning in the deep.

The waters vanish.
The land is a mirage.
We do not drown—just twist
in agony, suspended in
the dank atmosphere.

Deep, deep in my psyche, I constantly feared that more
significant others in my life would suddenly die. I would
have to learn to trust the universe all over again.

I had handled the accident by mentally arranging the
tragedy neatly and logically into a system of religious
propositions. The ordering certainly was very helpful on
one level, but clearly it was not salve enough for the deep
wounds. The responsibility I felt as a professional lay
minister had led me to try to model a role of strength during
adversity. I never allowed myself the proper time for the
deep grief that inevitably follows such a loss. The deep
wounding and the lack of proper grief time caused great
inner conflict. I felt like a tightrope walker:

Like a tightrope walker I
teeter seesaw fashion
on the brink of the precipice
striving desperately for balance.

The line is razor sharp
So easy to get cut by
slipping either way.
Help! Give me a pole.

   "Thy rod and thy staff they comfort me."

I stand at the Cross section
between nature/spirit. It dissects me—
while holding the self
horizontal and vertical.

One doesn't get over panic attacks like a case of the flu.
Twenty years ago there was less knowledge about how to
treat anxiety. Basically I learned, by trial and error, that any
giving into the fear of an attack only heightened the tension.
John Wilson, an ordained Baptist pastor and psychiatrist at

11

Vanderbilt University, helped me understand that it was necessary to continue with the tasks of daily life, regardless of the panic. A long struggle with these attacks finally led me to the realization that there was no way to conquer the problem other than to do what is suggested in the popular vernacular expression, "keep on keeping on," or in language of the open road, "keep on truckin' on."

There is no question that Richard's death and the pressures of graduate school triggered the fear of powerlessness. I inherited the genetic tendency toward high blood pressure from my father. But truly, the process involving the inner connections between my wounded psyche and my body remains a mystery to this day. Furthermore, I had to learn to "let go" of my need for all possible logical answers.

Recovery

Recovery was slow. The panic was persistent and severe. I followed my intuition and clung to anything positive that brought relief. If I caught myself starting to play "catastrophe," I would consciously stop the game. Credit for helping me keep my balance during those early years belongs to a magnificent Scottish Terrier dog named Champion Caritas Graylinden, C.D. "Tas" more than lived up to his Latin name *caritas* which means "benevolent love." Looking back, I think it was important to have had this small creature dependent on me each day. We had fun together as I showed him to his Championship, and he earned a Companion Dog Obedience certificate. I joked that the dog earned titles and degrees much faster than his owner. Besides, Tas consistently was affectionate no matter what my moods, no matter how great my anxiety.

I read poetry but I stopped reading Sylvia Plath and Anne Sexton when I discovered they had committed suicide. I wrote my own poetry. Anger, unresolved grief, fear, and my theology poured out in images onto paper. In Lent, 1964 I wrote this verse:

> I am belted in—constricting myself
> To keep from swishing crazily
> Around like a balloon that has
> Lost air and falls
> A broken ribbon to earth.

12

The hand extended shouts,
"Loose your safety belt—
Dare to rise again to life!"
Reaching for the hook I sense
Rain drops misting the air.

I am a tree whose roots
Long parched from drought
Gulps greedily new found water,
Until satiated drinks evenly and
Slowly unfolds to green.

The oasis is no mirage
Standing on The Rock
I gaze at the terrible,
beautiful sea echoing a song,
"The battle o'er, the victory won. . ."

Anxiety that came in waves was exorcised by images of healing water. I used my studies to explore the riches of the many baptismal traditions within the Christian faith family. Making the spiritual pilgrimage each year from Lent to Easter, with its powerful liturgical images of death to life, became much more than the traditional churchly rite of winter. And one spring season I must have sung a thousand times, "On Christ the solid rock I stand, all other ground is sinking sand, all other ground is sinking sand." I sang that particular hymn refrain over and over, banging my fist on the steering wheel and dash of my car.

During a particularly stressful period, a friend's mother said to me, "Hang on to Jesus; Diedra, hang on to Jesus." How does one "hang on to Jesus?" That instruction did not seem proper for a university-trained church historian. I stopped myself from processing this idea through the content of my studies and in desperation did just what she suggested. I hung on. I hung on to the promises of God that I learned as a child, to the claims for healing and new life by the Old and New Testament writers, to the testimonies of faith taught to me by seminary teachers, and most of all to the story of the resurrection and post resurrection traditions. The texts and tunes of hymns became an important part of my recovery; the music of Bach and Brahms nourished my soul. The mysterious reason for

13

suffering became absorbed into the greater reality of a gracious spiritual presence that always seemed to be there pulling me toward new life.

My friends looked at me quizzically the day I announced to them that I was a saint. They did not understand the context in which I felt a strong, real and intimate bond with the faithful ones, those Christian folk whom we call "the saints." The stories of suffering, transformation, and ministry of Christians through the ages strengthened and enlightened the perception of my journey. The saints had done what I was also trying to be about; *they persisted in the religious vision despite the problems and discouragements of everyday living.* My friends were also the saints, the people of God, who sustained me with their hospitality and generous love through those difficult years.

There have been no panic attacks in twelve years. I knew the turn had come when suddenly one day I realized that I had bought a bright orange car to replace the succession of dark blues I had been driving. I have remarried and life is extremely rewarding and full of promise. I would never want to go back through those years, but I would not trade the person that was forged from that crucible. You see, God had a secret for me. Out of the confusion and discontinuity of those years came an explosion of new life.

> Here and now I will do a new
>   thing;
>   this moment it will break from
>   the bud.
>   Can you not perceive it?
>   (Isaiah 43:18-19, NEB)

Evergreen trees became an important symbol for me of the constancy of life even within seasonal changes. The biblical writers said some beautiful things about God and trees and us. These words from Isaiah seemed especially powerful:

> The wretched and the poor look for water and find none,
>   their tongues are parched with thirst;
> but I the LORD will give them an answer,
> I, the God of Israel, will not forsake them.
> I will open rivers among the sand-dunes
>   and wells in the valleys;

14

I will turn the wilderness into pools
and dry land into springs of water;
I will plant cedars in the wastes,
and acacia and myrtle and wild olive;
the pine shall grow on the barren heath
side by side with fir and box,
that men may see and know,
may once for all give heed and understand
that the LORD himself has done this,
   that the Holy One of Israel has performed it.
(Isaiah 41:17-20, NEB)

Isaiah uses various evergreen trees as appropriate symbols for hope in the midst of dryness. What a powerful image for our imaginations to think of God planting cedar trees in the barren wastelands and opening rivers among the sand-dunes in our lives.

In one of the most beautiful and comforting images in the Bible, Yahweh declares to Hosea, "I am the pine tree that shelters you. . ." (Hosea 14:8, NEB). I held onto the promises of God and they were true. The powerful, creative love of God shelters us during times of tragedy and God's love is there at the starting points where new life begins again. Within all the changes and turning points of life, the pine tree remains evergreen and reminds us of the steadfast, caring nature of God through all seasons.

Discussion Questions

List and share together possible answers to these four questions. Remember that no one set of religious propositions neatly package the experience of human suffering. Each person's experience with suffering in relationship to the Christian community will be uniquely valid. No struggle with suffering is too minor or too small not to be considered. Every person is a valuable member of the community of faith and every struggle is worthy of attention from the healing, caring community we call the church.

1. In 1710, the philosopher Leibniz coined the word *theodicy* as a term to be used whenever thinkers try to justify the fact that evil exists in a world of divine justice. Writers on issues of theodicy ask why evil exists in a world created by a good God. What is the position of the author on the question of theodicy?

2. Do you believe that God causes suffering? What is the distinction drawn by Leslie D. Weatherhead between God *intentionally* willing a disaster or the possibility that God *allows* tragic circumstances to occur within the natural order? Is it God's will that we suffer?

3. What were some of the ways in which the author drew upon the resources of the Christian community to help her work through suffering? What are some of the religious images that she found valuable? Do you find some of these same resources to be helpful? Discuss those images that speak to you in times of suffering.

4. Christians, as individuals, suffer through such things as illness, death, or estrangement in relationships. Suffering also occurs because persons are a part of a group. For example, one's race, gender, age or ideas may lead to painful experiences. Members may wish to write down one example of either type of suffering that has occurred in their own lives and share it with the group. Together give and receive your own stories!

Spiritual Exercises

Exercise I: Designing Clothes for Suffering

Contemporary poet Adrienne Rich describes three friends who are suffering. The poet uses the image of costume to show how three different women communicate their personal hurt before the world.[6]

Women

My three sisters are sitting
on rocks of black obsidian.
For the first time, in this light, I can see
who they are.

My first sister is sewing her costume for the
procession.
She is going as the Transparent Lady
and all her nerves will be visible.

My second sister is also sewing,
at the seam over her heart which has never
healed entirely.
At last, she hopes, this tightness in her
chest will ease.

My third sister is gazing
at a dark-red crust spreading westward far
out on the sea.
Her stockings are torn but she is beautiful.

Obsidian stones are hard, volcanic glass whose surface features are naturally reflective. In the light of the reflections of these beautiful stones, the poet sees deep into the suffering in her friends' lives.

Clothes made of sackcloth were worn in biblical times as a visible sign of suffering. Today we also wear open badges of our pain. In some cultures arm bands are commonly used as a sign of mourning. Beyond the signifying of individual

---

[6] "Women" is reprinted from *The Fact of a Doorframe, Poems Selected and New 1950-1984*, by Adrienne Rich, by permission of W. W. Norton & Company, Inc. Copyright © 1984 by Adrienne Rich. Copyright © 1975, 1978 by W. W. Norton & Company, Inc. Copyright © 1981 by Adrienne Rich.

deaths, the ribbons worn during the Atlanta child slayings and a "ribbon" stretched around the Pentagon on the 40th anniversary of the 1945 bombing of Hiroshima were also badges of pain.

We protectively clothe ourselves when we suffer. Very often that mental clothing is quite visible to family and friends. Each of these three women in Rich's poem is making or wearing clothing that reflects her attitude toward the suffering she undergoes.

It is interesting for me to think about the *imaginary* type of clothing I wore after the accident in Mexico. Although I was not ordained clergy at the time, I most certainly wrapped myself symbolically in a pulpit robe. The religious garb protected my body from the outside world. When I was wrapped in a preaching robe, curious eyes could not see what was happening inside me. The pulpit robe, whose origins are in the medieval university, symbolizes in the church the proclamation of the Gospel Word and probably is a very good image for the brave front I tried to construct in my professional life.

I have a battered friend who wears (in my imagination, of course) a lovely business suit of meshed mail. This suit looks like a stunning Paris creation, but it is designed of a mesh fabric comprised of flexible, small, overlapping metal rings and scales. Her professional mail suit protects her feelings nearly as well as the body armor of the knights of old. The abuse occurred several years before, but this woman still bears the inner scars of fear. The beauty of the suit hides the bruises. The fabric keeps new relationships at a distance.

In reality, of course, there is no such meshed mail suit—just as I did not literally wrap myself in a preaching robe. New self-discovery may be possible, however, by describing or drawing the type of symbolic clothing we wear when we are suffering.

What kind of garments do you think you wear during times of suffering? Do you choose an outfit that protects and veils you? Does your covering shelter and screen you from those outside? Or is your suffering visible and transparent through the materials you choose?

I'd like you to try to imagine the kind of symbolic clothing that you actually wear when you are in a situation involving suffering. You might wear one piece of clothing—a hat, for example—or you might wear a whole outfit. The type of material that you choose is also important.

You might even do a color sketch using paper and crayons. Thus, you will mentally design your suffering outfit. Be honest with yourself. Share what you wish with others in your study group. Are you pleased with the symbolic clothing you have made? Would you like to try another kind of clothing the next time you are suffering? What do you think is the ideal set of clothing to help you cope with pain?

Jesus tells us that we should not be anxious about the clothes that cover our body. We might as well not be anxious about what we shall wear tomorrow, he says, for tomorrow will look after itself and "each day has troubles enough of its own." We are told to set our minds on God's kingdom and God's justice before everything else and "all the rest will come to you as well" (Matthew 6:28-34).

Does this scripture have something to say to us about the invisible clothes that we wear today or worry about wearing tomorrow in case there is a crisis?

Close with the reading of the parable of the sheep and the goats in Matthew 25:31-46. Jesus has strong words about the responsibilities of those who follow him. Jesus reminds us that some suffering people come to us for help and they wear no clothes at all. Sometimes, of course, our mission is quite literally to clothe those who have no clothing. In other cases, however, the burden of suffering may strip persons of all defenses, leaving them feeling vulnerable and naked. The sufferers will be wearing clothing on their bodies that we can see; however, we may be advised to look deeper to the scars that the reflection of obsidian casts before us.

(This prayer is a revision of an ancient prayer from a medieval primer. The primers were small prayer books provided for lay people to use for the daily prayers and on special occasions. This prayer was probably from the memorial of the cross at the Good Friday liturgy. Conclude your session with it.)

Lord Jesus Christ, Son of the living God, we pray you to set your passion, cross, and death between your judgment and our souls, now and in the hour of our death. Give mercy and grace to the living; pardon and rest to the dead;

to your holy Church peace and concord; and to us sinners everlasting life and glory. Amen.[7]

Exercise II: Poetic Imaging

Writing verse and reading the poetry of others was a medium of healing for the author. Exploring the images that best expressed her suffering became an important source of power. Expressing anger and grief through poetry both cushioned the pain and revealed the depth of the hurt. Poetic images enable the sufferer to look more boldly at the pain while at the same time opening up a channel for healing grace.

The study group is invited to search during this next week for those poetic images that both reveal and heal. Lois B. Robbins suggests that we probably do a lot more imaging than we realize.[8] She recommends carrying a small notebook to write down or draw anything that pops into the mind. The most important time, she believes, to be aware of your inner images is when you first wake up in the morning. Many people keep writing materials next to their beds in case a thought or dream image surfaces during the night. "The more you snag images, respect them, and give them credence and life, the more they will reward you with profusion," thinks Lois Robbins.[9] As we grow in the process of expressing our images in verse our very selves become transformed.

1. Carry a notebook this week and snag any images that hurt or heal.

2. Toward the end of the week, try to make connections between the images you have perceived and what they represent in your life. For example, the poet Denise Levertov connected hidden grief with the depth of a mineshaft. These verses are from a longer poem entitled "Dwellers at the Hermitage."[10]

---

[7] *The Book of Common Prayer of the Episcopal Church in the United States* (New York: The Church Hymnal Corporation and Seabury Press, 1977), p. 282.

[8] Lois B. Robbins, *Waking Up in the Age of Creativity* (Sante Fe, New Mexico: Bear & Company, 1985), pp. 122-123.

[9] *Ibid.*

[10] Denise Levertov, *Candles in Babylon* (New York: New Directions Publishing Corporation, 1982), p. 3. Copyright © 1982 by Denise Levertov. Used by permission.

Grief sinks and sinks
into the old mineshaft
under the house,
how deep, who knows.
When they have need
for it, it's there.

3. Discover your own mental pictures. What do these images represent? Finally, connect the mental pictures and what they signify into verse. Some of the best images are short and to the point. Alice Walker captures feelings of rage in these few words:[11]

The silence between your words
rams into me
like a sword.

4. Start the next session together by reading the poems.[12] Only share, however, if you feel comfortable doing so. Discuss how members felt while finding their images.

Spiritual Exercise III

If members of the group would like to try a further spiritual exercise, a valuable resource for meditating on the scriptures may be found in a book by Carolyn Stahl, *Opening to God, Guided Imagery Meditation on Scripture* (Nashville: The Upper Room, 1977). Especially useful here is Exercise 23, "Letting Go of Anxiety—Accepting God's Provisions."

---

[11] Alice Walker, "Rage," *Revolutionary Petunias & Other Poems* (New York: Harcourt Brace Javonovich, Inc., 1973), p. 61. Used by permission.

[12] The leader may wish to explore some further images with the group. The following suggestions are all found in *The Norton Anthology of Literature by Women*, Sandra M. Gilbert and Susan Gubar, eds. (New York: W. W. Norton & Company, 1985): Ruth Stone, "Second Hand Coat"; Gwendolyn Brooks, "We Real Cool"; May Swenson, "Bleeding"; Denise Levertov, "The Wings" and "Divorcing"; Adrienne Rich, "Power"; Audre Lorde, "Coal"; and Margaret Atwood "[You fit into me]".

Further Reading

Ebinger, Mary Ritzman. "Alone." *Beginnings and Beyond: A Collection of Playlets for United Methodist Women.* #4568, $1.75*

"Alone" is a play about two United Methodist Women whose husbands die. A chart on ways people grieve, a list of resources, and discussion questions are included. The bibliography is excellent and highly recommended.

Gilbert, Sandra M. and Susan Gubar, eds. *The Norton Anthology of Literature by Women, The Tradition in English.* New York: W. W. Norton & Company, 1985.

A single volume of literary works by women from the fourteenth to the twentieth centuries.

Hick, John. *Evil and the God of Love.* New York: Harper & Row, 1977.

A very important theological treatment on theodicy.

Kubler-Ross, Elizabeth. *To Live until We Say Goodby.* Englewood Cliffs, New Jersey: Prentice-Hall, Inc., 1978.

True stories of courage in the face of death.

Kushner, Harold S. *When Bad Things Happen to Good People.* New York: Avon Books, 1981.

A Jewish treatment of theodicy.

Weatherhead, Leslie D. *The Will of God.* Nashville: Abingdon Press, 1976.

Weatherhead's five lectures, first published in 1944, still speak to the issue of the relationship between suffering and the will of God.

Willimon, William H. *Sighing for Eden, Sin, Evil and the Christian Faith.* Nashville: Abingdon Press, 1985.

A popular restatement of John Hick's classic work on theodicy.

Books for Children and Youth

Allen Terry, ed. *The Whispering Wind—Poetry by Young American Indians.* Garden City, New York: Doubleday, Inc., 1968.

Bontemps, Arna, ed. *American Negro Poetry.* New York: Hill and Wang, 1963.

Orgel, Doris. *The Mulberry Music.* New York: Harper & Row, 1971.
A young teen works through a parent's death.

---

* Available from the Service Center, 7820 Reading Road, Cincinnati, Ohio 45237.

Chapter II

THE CARMELITE MONASTERY OF THE INCARNATION, AVILA, SPAIN, A.D. 1554

One of the great storytellers of our time, Elie Wiesel, tells a rabbinic tale which points to the importance of narrative for the religious life.

> When the great Rabbi Israel Baal Shem-Tov saw misfortune threatening the Jews it was his custom to go into a certain part of the forest to meditate. There he would light a fire, say a special prayer, and the miracle would be accomplished and the disaster averted.
>
> Later, when his disciple, the celebrated Magid of Mezeritch, had occasion, for the same reason, to intercede with heaven, he would go to the same place in the forest and say: "Master of the Universe, listen! I do not know how to light the fire, but I am still able to say the prayer." And again the miracle would be accomplished.
>
> Still later, Rabbi Moshe-Leib of Sassov, in order to save his people once more, would go into the forest and say: "I do not know how to light the fire, I do not know the prayer, but I know the place and this must be sufficient." It was sufficient and the miracle was accomplished.
>
> Then it fell to Rabbi Israel of Rizhin to overcome misfortune. Sitting in his armchair, his head in his hands, he spoke to God: I cannot even find the place in the forest. All I can do is to tell the story, and this must be sufficient." And it was sufficient.[1]

The stories of faith, as told in the biblical texts and in the examples of Christian people throughout the centuries, give grace to the contemporary Church by providing an interpretive framework for such age-old questions as the meaning of suffering. One of the great resources available to help the present Christian community deal with suffering is found in

---

[1] Elie Wiesel, *The Gates of the Forest,* transl. by Frances Frenaye (New York: Holt, Rinehart & Winston, Inc., 1968). Used by permission.

the stories of its saints.[2] Saints are not necessarily long suffering or even lovable people but rather they are ordinary Christians who are so totally grasped by the religious vision of God that this vision becomes the central motivating factor in their lives.[3] This religious fact changes and transforms the lives of these people so totally that others are led to glimpse the value of that vision for their own lives.[4]

A prophetic warning is sounded however, in Wiesel's Rabbinic lore. How easy it is for succeeding generations to forget the traditions of the past! A later generation of rabbis could not remember the location of the special place for meditation, were unable to recall how to light the fire and even the powerful prayer was lost. All that was left was the story about the great Rabbi Israel Baal Shem-Tov. Nevertheless, there was such power in the telling of the traditional account that the tale was sufficient. But what if the story itself is lost? Where will the power then be found to avert the danger?

---

[2] The term "saint" is used here in three ways: first, in the general biblical sense of the people of God (Romans 1:7). The saints are referred to in the Bible as "the faithful ones" (Ephesians 1:1). Every Christian is called to be a saint (*hagios*) in this general sense of the term.

In addition, there are those believers who exhibit a special character of sanctity or holiness. A sanctified person, that is, one who exhibits the character of holiness, may come from any time period (including our own), from widely varying cultures, and from any denomination. Lawrence Cunningham, who is a specialist in hagiography (the lives of saints), defines the saintly personality as one that exhibits grace for the benefit of others. Cunningham, quoting Paul Tillich's words, declares that a saint is a "sign-event."

Historically the word "saint" has been used in a third and more restricted sense. Until the tenth century, persons were proclaimed "saints" simply by listening to the voice of the people. After the tenth century, the Catholic tradition began to develop official procedures for designating persons as saints. This official process is called canonization. The term "saint" is *not* used in this third sense in this book. We call Teresa of Avila a saint because she is one of the "faithful ones," and because she exhibits grace for others, although Teresa is also officially canonized.

[3] Cunningham writes in *The Meaning of Saints* (San Francisco: Harper & Row Publishers, 1980), p. 73, "Every Christian is, in a certain sense, a saint; but when a Christian's love and faith is such that it becomes a sign for others who are grasped by the power and the creativity of that faith or love, then the person is a saint in a more specific and concrete way."

[4] Cunningham, p. 65.

24

Protestant Christians are in danger of losing the stories of the tradition. Adults and children alike have few Christian heroes from the past to inspire and interpret the Gospel. Where are we told about the lives of those concrete historical people whose living vision can challenge and inspire us?

Spiritual amnesia seems to be particularly severe in the case of the experiences of women in the Church. It is mind wrenching to think about the vast number of women who have been Christians in the almost 2000 years of church story and how few of their names that we know. In the decade of the sixties, I went through years of course work in both seminary and graduate school and I cannot recall the name of a single women assigned to be studied. Thanks to the feminist movement and to the increasing numbers of women scholars in the field of religion, there has been a rediscovery of women leaders through the centuries. One woman's name that has become increasingly familiar to U.S. Christians in recent years is that of the 16th century reformer Teresa of Avila.

Teresa of Avila

The suffering and courage of a 16th century nun named Teresa of Avila is a story whose telling may be helpful for the spiritual pilgrimage of contemporary Christians.[5] In 1515, two years before Martin Luther tacked a challenge to medieval Catholicism on the door of Wittenberg Church, a girl child was born to Don and Doña de Cepeda in Avila, a well-to-do cloth merchant known for his charitable deeds. Teresa's mother, Doña Beatriz de Ahumada, was the second wife of the Don. She was married to him at fourteen and was dead at thirty-three, having given birth to ten children.

---

[5] Most of the information on the life of Teresa is taken from her autobiographical works including *The Book of Her Life, Spiritual Testimonies, Soliloquies,* and *The Interior Castle.* Unless otherwise designated, the information on Teresa will come from *The Book of Her Life* in *The Collected Works of St. Teresa of Avila,* vol. 1, trans. Kieran Kavanaugh and Otilio Rodriguez (Washington, D.C.: ICS publications, Institute of Carmelite Studies, 1976).

Teresa was twelve when her mother died. She was reported to have been a lively, outgoing girl who loved reading romantic novels about knights and chivalry. As far as we know, Teresa was physically healthy. When she was fourteen, Teresa reports that she spent her time dressing in her best clothes, experimenting with perfumes and tending to her hair and hands.

Fourteen-year-old girls in sixteenth century Spain seem much like adolescents in the twentieth century. Evidently Teresa was learning flirtatious sexual games, so her father became concerned with her relationship with male relatives. When her older sister married, Don Alonso sent Teresa, at the age of sixteen, to a boarding school run by Augustinian nuns. He was thinking quite sensibly that it was not good for her to be at home without a mother. The choice, however, did prove a cruel one, even though it was made out of genuine love and concern. Reflecting later, Teresa wrote, "When I left my father's house I felt the separation so keenly that the feeling will not be greater when I die, for it seemed that every bone in my body was being sundered."

So drastic was the change of life style from manor house to convent that the young girl experienced fainting spells and heart pains. Our bodies often ache at the places of severe disruptions. Teresa clearly suffered intense anxiety. Nevertheless she stayed and a friendly nun exerted gentle pressure on her to consider the religious life. Teresa wrote that while she could not yet persuade herself to become a nun, "I was, however, afraid to marry." The fear of marriage was not unrealistic, for Teresa had watched her mother go through a long series of debilitating pregnancies leading to a premature death. The conflict caused by the inner struggle for and against the life of "a religious" made her so sick that her father removed her from school. Don Alonzo boarded her with a fanatically pious widowed uncle who was given to discourses on the vanity of the world and the realities of eternal damnation. Teresa wrote the following words describing this period of struggle:

> I began to understand the truth I knew from childhood (the nothingness of all things, the vanity of the world, how it would soon come to an end) and to fear that if I were to die that I would

go to hell. And although my will did not completely incline to being a nun, I saw that the religious life was the best and safest state, and so little by little I decided to force myself to accept it.

Keep in mind that lifelong choices were narrow and limited for women in the sixteenth century. Basically, marriage or convent were the only two choices for a proper girl. For a young woman of independent spirit, and especially for one who demonstrated leadership ability, the convent was often the best alternative. Over her father's objections, Teresa took vows as a nun in the Carmelite monastery of the Incarnation. Don Alonzo provided a dowry just as he would have if she had chosen marriage.

Teresa claimed that she was happy. Yet the fainting spells increased. The "heart pains" were so severe that the attacks frightened witnesses. Teresa thought it was the food and the cloistered life-style that did injury to her health. A better clue might well be found in the passages where she spoke of the war that raged inside her. Teresa fought constant internal battles between "friendship with God and friendship with the world."

Inexplicably she developed symptoms of catalepsy, that is, her muscles became rigid and feeling was temporarily lost in her limbs. Once again she returned to her father's home and lost consciousness for so long that she was given last rites and her grave was prepared. She awoke four days later almost totally paralyzed. Eight months later, Teresa returned to the convent but she showed the effects of partial paralysis until middle-age.

Teresa vomited every morning for twenty years and could not take any food until afternoon. Eight years after the paralysis, Teresa recorded that she was almost never without pains and sometimes very severe ones, especially in the heart. Always there was a deep inner struggle or, as Teresa herself put it, "I voyaged on this tempestuous sea for almost twenty years."

As she was a member of a religious order and a contemplative community, it might be assumed that naturally Teresa would have found help in her prayer life. The opposite seems to have been the case. The physical paralysis she suffered seemed to have had its parallel in her spiritual life.[6] Indeed, during those unhappy years, she did pray a great deal. According to her autobiography, she spent hours composing agonizing prayers for inner peace. Periods of plodding through these petitions for God's help in her struggle were followed by times of "dryness." She must have felt somewhat like the poet Denise Levertov who penned these lines from a poem called, "Oblique Prayer":[7]

> . . . but gray,
> a place
> without clear outlines,
>
> the air
> heavy and thick
> the soft ground clogging
> my feet if I walk,
> sucking them downwards
> if I stand.

For a long time, she abandoned prayer altogether. Always honest with herself, Teresa wrote, "Discursive reflection is an extremely difficult thing to practice" and she confessed, "For some years, I was more anxious that the hour of prayer be over than I was to remain there."

At the age of thirty-nine, Teresa said of herself, "My soul now was tired." One day during that same year, she entered a small, private chapel at the convent. In this oratory, there was a statue of the wounded Christ borrowed for a feast day. Teresa's reaction upon studying the statue was instantaneous and dramatic. She wrote, "My heart broke." She threw herself on the ground before the religious statue and wept and wept. Sobbing before the figure of the wounded Christ, Teresa imagined that she, Teresa, was Mary Magdalene wiping the wounded Jesus with her tears; she would not rise until the Lord granted her the peace for which she so desperately longed. Teresa felt

---

[6] Catherine Romano, "A Psycho-Spiritual History of Teresa of Avila: A Woman's Perspective," in *Historical Roots, Ecumenical Routes,* ed. Matthew Fox (Santa Fe, New Mexico: Bear & Company, Inc., 1981), p. 268.

[7] An "oblique" prayer would veil or mask the real need so the petition is slanted or askew. Denise Levertov, "Oblique Prayer," *Oblique Prayers* (New York: New Directions Books, 1984), p. 82. Copyright © 1984 by Denise Levertov. Used by permission.

the spirit of Jesus suddenly present within her. She left the chapel with a deep and profound peace.

Transformation

Soon after this powerful religious experience, Teresa was given a copy of *The Confessions of St. Augustine*. "It seems," she wrote, "the Lord ordained this, because I had not tried to procure a copy, nor had I ever seen one." Teresa felt drawn to the life of Augustine because he confessed himself to be a sinner and she found great consolation in the stories of sinners whom God had brought back into relationship. Later she reflected on finding the *Confessions* in this way:

> As I began to read the *Confessions*, it seemed to me I saw myself in them. I began to commend myself very much to this glorious saint. When I came to the passage where he speaks about his conversion and read how he heard that voice in the garden, it only seemed to me, according to what I felt in my heart, that it was I the Lord called. I remained for a long time totally dissolved in tears and feeling within myself utter distress and weariness. Oh, how a soul suffers, God help me, by losing the freedom it should have in being itself; and what torments it undergoes! I marvel now at how I could have lived in such great affliction. May God be praised who gave me the life to rise up from a death so deadly.[8]

Teresa, the sick nun, began to find comfort and hope in the faith story of Augustine, a Christian who lived eleven centuries before her in a very different time and culture. In just the same way, Beth E. Rhude could write in 1980, "Teresa's autobiography, soliloquies, prayers, reflections and letters seemed at first to be so far from my own life. Yet, the more I read her story, peppered with prayer in such a way it is not always easy to tell when she is talking to herself, to the reader, or to God, the more appreciation and intimacy I felt with this woman."[9] Thus the Spirit works through our stories, giving courage and hope to the next

---

[8] Kieran Kavanaugh and Otilio Rodriguez, transls., *Collected Works of St. Teresa of Avila, Volume One* (Washington, D.C.: ICS Publications, 1976), p. 73. Used by permission.

[9] Beth E. Rhude, "Enjoying God, Teresa of Avila (1515-1582)," in *Live the Questions Now, The Interior Life*, ed., Beth E. Rhude (Women's Division Board of Global Ministries, The United Methodist Church, 1980), p. 64.

generations as Augustine did to Teresa, Teresa to Beth Rhude, Rhude to. . .[10]

Immediately following this experience, Teresa focused once again on her prayer life. "The Lord taught me more in the next four months than in the last seventeen years of prayer life," reflected Teresa. From that moment, she began to practice a new *method* of prayer. She no longer struggled with the long, rambling petitions that principally involved her intellect. Teresa called upon all her senses as she freely used the religious imagery that welled up within herself.

Teresa would set aside a prayer time before retiring for the night. Following some centering exercises typical of the period she would picture Jesus in scenes from the Gospels. Then through the power of her imagination, Teresa put herself in the scene with Jesus. In the beginning she had most success picturing Jesus by himself in situations of suffering. An early favorite was Jesus, agonizing alone, in the Garden of Gethsemane. All his male companions were asleep. Teresa put herself into the scene. "He had to accept me," she fantasized, as she sought somehow to help her Lord in need. She wanted to wipe away Jesus' sweat, but she never dared touch him, even if it were only in her imagination.

Prayer assumed the form of an intimate sharing between friends. Casting herself into the biblical scenes seemed to establish a living bond of communication between Teresa and Jesus. This sense of intimacy would lead eventually to mystical states in which Teresa would feel a complete bonding with Jesus. She concluded the prayer time by commending herself to God before going to sleep.

As she developed this method, Teresa focused on prayer scenes involving Jesus with other women in the Bible. She

---

[10] In her book *Diving Deep and Surfacing, Women Writers on Spiritual Quest*, (Boston: Beacon Press, 1980), p. 1, Carol Christ (pronounced Kríst) undertakes an important analysis of the spiritual experiences of women. Christ contends that women's stories have not been told and without stories women are lost when it comes to making the important decisions of life. A woman who is isolated from feminine faith stories, "does not learn to value her struggles, to celebrate her strengths, to comprehend her pain." And without stories a woman cannot fully understand herself for she is "alienated from those deeper experiences of self and world that have been called spiritual or religious."

liked to play the Samaritan woman who did not flinch before the Lord's judgment of her sexual life.[11] Over and over, Teresa played the parts of both Mary and Martha. She declared that without Martha the Lord would have had no dinner; without Mary there would be no contemplative life. Teresa always commended her daily life to God following these experiences.

Two years of utilizing this new prayer method transformed Teresa from a sickly, unhappy, suffering woman to one whose growth in wholeness and health astonished her community. Gradually mental petitions reentered her prayers along with the quiet periods of the prayer scenes.

Teresa continued to amaze her community. At age forty-one, after twenty years in one religious house, she became increasingly impatient with the spiritual laxity of the Spanish religious orders. Through the act in which she was prayerfully role playing Mary and Martha, Teresa had arrived at a compelling insight—the conviction that the life of prayer and the active life should be joined together. She decided, therefore, to join the forces of the Counter-Reformation. Teresa left the convent, without permission of her superiors, for the purpose of restoring spirituality to the Carmelite communities in Spain.

And what a Reformer! This formerly immobilized woman began traveling throughout Spain under the hardest of conditions. According to historian Roland Bainton, "Time after time, she traveled in covered wagons, through torrid heat and congealing cold over roads dusty, muddy or frozen, over fords in ferries where the cable might break and send the scow careening over rapids until beached on the sandbank." To dramatize the reformation, she often dressed in sackcloth, wore a horse blanket for a coat and went shoeless. The Reformers were called the Discalced Carmelites, which means literally "the shoeless ones." Teresa nicknamed her companions in reform "the butterflies." She called her opponents "the grasshoppers." Through her efforts, Teresa founded fifteen Discalced

---

[11] Roland H. Bainton, *Women of the Reformation from Spain to Scandinavia* (Minneapolis, Minnesota: Augsburg Publishing House, 1977), p. 50.

religious houses for women. Interestingly, she named them for Joseph, for she felt that he should also get credit for raising the boy Jesus.[12]

There was great opposition from the church's hierarchy to the work of Teresa and her two companions in reform, Gratian and St. John of the Cross. As the tension mounted, John was imprisoned in solitary confinement by the Inquisition for nine months and beaten daily. He managed to escape by loosening the screw in his cell lock, and letting himself down out of a window with a rope made from his bedclothes. Before he was briefly imprisoned, Gratian ate only hard boiled eggs to ward off poisoning. Teresa hid while she made a formal appeal to King Philip II on behalf of the reformers. The Papal Nuncio wrote this assessment of Teresa:

> A restless, gadabout, disobedient, contumacious woman who promulgates pernicious doctrine under pretence of devotion. She leaves her cloisters against the orders of her superiors contrary to the decrees of the Council of Trent. She is ambitious and teaches theology as if she were a doctor of the Church in spite of St. Paul's prohibition.[13]

In spite of the Nuncio's ire, Teresa and the other reformers eventually achieved the goal of two separate Carmelite orders. In addition, she also wrote four books while traveling and establishing the fifteen Reformed religious houses.

Positive and Negative Self-Talk

In the earlier days of her novitiate, Teresa was attracted to the suffering of a nun with a disease which caused holes in her abdomen making "obstructions in such a way that she had to eject through them what she ate." The nun soon died. Teresa observed that other members of the convent feared that affliction. "As for myself," Teresa writes, "I envied her patience." Curiously, Teresa thought it would gain her eternal "brownie points" if she too showed patience through suffering and she even asked God to give her illnesses. The Lord seemed to do just what Teresa had

---

[12] Bainton, pp. 55-56.
[13] Bainton, p. 56.

requested, and she became painfully sick for a three year period. Until her conversion in the chapel of the convent, Teresa adopted a Christian life-style that might be characterized as that of a "suffering martyr." After the change in her religious perspective and her health, Teresa analyzes herself with uncommon honesty; "Since I am so sickly, I have always been tied down without being worth anything until I determined to pay no attention to the body or to my health . . . for afterward when I wasn't so cared for and pampered, I had much better health."

Teresa's decision as a young adult to imitate the health as well as the pious attitudes of an older nun had enormous implications for her well being. What is revealed in these autobiographical words was an unconscious commitment to the image of herself as a sick person.

Teresa's decision reminds me of a case study I read recently of a sixty-four-year-old American woman named Viola, who at the time she changed physicians had been severely depressed for two years.[14] Before the onset of the depression, Viola has been an active, involved woman who prided herself on her ability as a homemaker. A marriage crisis led to symptoms that put her in the psychiatric ward of a general hospital. She had undergone shock therapy for the depression and was taking a number of tranquilizing drugs. Viola seemed eager to convince her new therapist that she was, in fact, extremely depressed and that no therapy could help her.

Like Teresa, Viola accepted her identity as a person who was sick and depressed. She refused to hold more positive perceptions of herself. She talked to herself as if she were sick and thus locked herself into an identity of failure. Since she saw herself as a sick person, Viola negated any possibility of change. She could not be helped because she said to herself in a hundred different ways, "I can't do anything to help myself because I am so depressed." Doesn't that sound like what Teresa might have said to herself, "I can't do anything to help myself because I am so sick"?

---

[14] Ronald C. Harshman, "I Don't Have to Be Sick to Be Somebody," in *What Are You Doing? How People Are Helped Through Reality Therapy*, ed., Naomi Glasser (New York: Harper & Row, 1980), pp. 89-95.

Viola's suffering was, in its own way, an attempt to fulfill the need to belong and to be loved. But she needed to be taught a better and healthier way to accomplish the same goals. Viola learned a more positive self-image. She concluded, "I don't have to be sick to be somebody." She had recovered from the severe depression with a healthier and more productive self-concept.

These two women, one from the sixteenth century and one from the twentieth, are soul sisters in suffering. Poet Erica Jong describes this mental self-flagellation in contemporary images:[15]

> The best slave
> does not need to be beaten.
> She beats herself.
>
> Not with a leather whip,
> or with sticks or twigs,
> not with a blackjack
> or a billyclub,
> but with the fine whip
> of her own tongue
> & the subtle beating
> of her mind
> against her mind.

Teresa decided to begin ignoring her health problems and discovered that she felt much better when she was less pampered. In a sense, Teresa's ability to look at herself more positively came as the result of the focused role playing in her prayer life. Whenever Teresa put herself prayerfully into the role of biblical people, she was unconsciously trying out or modeling a new, more positive self image.[16]

The mental picture she held of herself, a picture that

---

[15] Erica Jong, "Alcestis on the Poetry Circuit," *Half-Lives* (New York: Holt, Rinehart and Winston, Publishers, 1973), reprinted in *The Norton Anthology*, p. 2357. Used by permission.

[16] Teresa herself would never have considered a therapeutic interpretation of her healing. She believed that her new health came from the healing activity of God. The comparison with Viola is not to suggest otherwise. It was meditative prayer that proved to be the vehicle through which God healed Teresa.

produced such a limping self-image modeled after the long-suffering nun in her past, slowly changed. Teresa's internal self-talk became more positive.[17] The belief in herself as a sickly person, full of self-pity and unable to function, gave way to new confident attitudes about herself. As she tried to ignore the pains, Teresa began to see herself more like the Samaritan woman who was so gutsy that when Jesus reminded her of her loose life, the woman did not flinch but called him a prophet. Teresa joyously exclaims, "Oh, how many times do I recall the living water that the Lord told the Samaritan woman about! And I am so very fond of that gospel passage."

Indeed, Teresa really did become like the efficient administrator, Martha, as she founded and raised money for the building of reformed convents. She also remained true to Martha's sister, Mary, and for Teresa, prayer and meditation provided both the power and the authority for her mission. Teresa of Avila died a peaceful death on 4 October 1582 at sixty-seven years of age.

Transforming Power for Today

Courage to try a new method of communicating with God transformed Teresa's life and changed the direction of her church. Teresa, prostrate before a statue crying for inner peace at age thirty-nine, could never have imagined that Christians would be interested in her struggles many centuries later. Indeed, we are interested because, quite literally, Teresa "hung on" to Jesus. She put her arms around the statue of the wounded Christ and hung on. With determined grit, she prayed and stayed until Jesus answered her cries. Teresa left the chapel with inner peace for the first time since childhood. The "amazing grace" of God provided the converting moment so needed in her life.

---

[17] Teresa belongs to the Christian mystical tradition of the high middle-ages. She must always be seen within the context of her times. Teresa may be classified as an *alumbrados,* a member of the Spanish "illuminist" movement who stressed a spirituality consisting of mental prayer, inwardness, and contemplation. The theory that negative emotional feelings can be altered toward positive attitudes by changing our internal self-talk is a twentieth century concept represented by the work of Albert Ellis.

Change was not instantaneous, but Teresa persisted by developing a new prayer life. She learned from experience that the purpose of prayer is to transform the one praying. Effective prayer was the positive force that changed Teresa. Prayer is one holy tool that can help free us from doubt, anxiety and conflict. The experiences of Teresa also point to the power of the imagination in our prayer lives. Her life suggests that the freedom to experiment in the area of prayer styles is a valid enterprise for Christians. For Teresa, the capacity to reform church and world depended on this foundation. In her case, it was this transforming prayer that led her to seek renewal in a larger cause.

Teresa of Avila never looked back. This sixteenth-century Christian woman deserves our salute and the Church should pay careful attention to her faith story. Although Teresa was plagued with ill health all her life, this weak and sickly woman became a strong, vigorous individual. This woman with no power achieved miracles as a reformer. She attained the status of a great writer without the benefit of a formal education. All these accomplishments occurred in an environment that was not hospitable to women leaders. In theologian Paul Tillich's words, Teresa of Avila's life is a Christian sign-event.

Despite her struggles, Teresa was so grasped by the religious vision that it transformed her life and led her to pursue a wider religious vocation. There was an emotional shift in the center of her being from constant self-concern to what William James has called "the feeling of being in a wider life." This widening horizon gave her a "yes, yes" rather than a "no, no" to life which, in turn, led to an increase of self-forgetting charity.[18]

God calls each of us, Teresa-Diedra-*And Each Reader Of This Book*, to take charge of whatever may be our suffering and to look for help in the resources of the community of faith. For her first forty-one years, Teresa was an ordinary (and sickly) sixteenth-century woman. The same spiritual power that transformed Teresa in mid-life is available for Christians today and at any age along the religious journey.

Within the limits of each individual's personal problems, God asks us to work for the welfare of our neighbor and toward *shalom*, the vision of a just and peaceful world. One of the oldest and soundest pieces of Christian folk-wisdom is that if persons truly want to stop suffering they will go help others in greater need. Teresa learned that helping others and working hard for a just cause can be the best therapy in the world. By the grace of God, whatever our struggles, we can all learn to sing, *"Hallelujah, Anyhow!"*

Discussion Questions

1. Christian "saints" mirror for the church the possibility of victorious life in the midst of suffering. The saints are the "noble" ones, not because they are purer or more righteous people than the rest of us. They are saints because they manage to continue living with a religious vision in the midst of formidable odds. They witness to the hope and the possibility of resurrected life.

How do the faith stories of Christians, past and present, help us to cope with our own suffering? Each group member might like to tell a favorite story about a saint whose life helped her in a time of trial. Share with each other some stories of Christian courage that have helped you through difficult times.

2. Sometimes we bring on our own suffering. In some ways Teresa was her own worst enemy. How did Teresa perpetuate her own pain? What brought about the change in her life? Have you ever been your own worst enemy?

3. How did Teresa overcome her suffering? Was the way she internally talked to herself important? What resources of the church helped her to become a new person?

4. Teresa arrived at the spiritual insight that the interior and the active life should be joined together. How did Teresa combine prayer and reformation? Can you think of examples of persons who combine the contemplative and active spiritual life in our present day?

5. Why do you think Teresa is called a "saint?" Do you agree with this judgment?

---

[18] The categories are Lawrence Cunningham's from *The Meaning of Saints*, pp. 65-69.

Spiritual Exercises

Spiritual Exercise I—Teresa's Prayer Method

Mark 7:24-30 contains the wonderful story of the persistent mother who begged Jesus to cure her child. The story is also told with some variations in Matthew 15:21-28. Why not try prayerfully to role-play this story, just as Teresa used to do.

Before you begin, here are some facts you should know about this story:

1. Jesus was probably in predominantly Gentile territory at the time of the incident.

2. The woman who found Jesus was a Phoenician from Syria. Her ancestors had been the Canaanites, ancient enemies of Israel. Matthew calls her a Canaanite woman.

3. According to Matthew, the disciples were annoyed at her persistent cries and urged Jesus to "send her away." Matthew records that, at first, Jesus himself ignored her pleas.

4. When Jesus finally responded to the woman, it was through the use of a literary device called a "riddle," which was used by people in his day when they engaged in "one-up-manship." To our ears, the riddle seems to be a very strange answer for someone in need. Jesus said, "Let the children be satisfied first; it is not fair to take the children's bread and throw it to the dogs." The meaning, however, seems clear enough. Jesus did not want to bother healing Gentiles. The reader should also know that the term "dogs" was a *very* derogatory Jewish expression used to put down foreigners and other unacceptable types of people. We can't tell this in English, but Jesus did soften the word "dogs" somewhat by using the diminutive form of the word in his own language so that the meaning in the scripture passage is actually "little dogs," or "puppies."

5. The mother in crisis was not put off either by the riddle or the use of the word "small dogs." She came right back at Jesus with the reply, "Sir, even the dogs under the table eat the children's scraps." The woman answered Jesus in the same manner that an intelligent male in his culture would have responded, that is, by finishing or concluding the riddle.

6. Mark's interpretation seems to be that Jesus was impressed by the woman's response and therefore agreed to heal her daughter. Matthew records that Jesus responded very positively, "Woman, what faith you have! Be it as you wish!"

7. It is interesting to speculate how this episode affected Jesus' understanding of his mission. Perhaps this persistent woman's story is an important link in the series of events that led the church to understand its mission.

Procedure for the Teresa Prayer

Members of the study group should sit in a comfortable position where they can feel as if they are alone and undisturbed. The leader may start with a short prayer asking God to open each person to the story of the brave Phoenician woman.

Start by explaining the texts as described above. Ask all participants to close their eyes and prayerfully imagine themselves into the role of the woman whose child was very ill.

Very, very slowly read the Mark account. Pause and then read the same story in Matthew. When you finish quietly ask the following questions, pausing between each one to allow time for meditation.

1. Your child is very sick. How do you feel as you search to find out where Jesus will spend the night?

2. As you look for Jesus, think about the reception you might expect to receive considering your cultural background and nationality.

3. What kind of emotional response do you have to the way the disciples reacted to your visit?

4. How do you feel when Jesus first ignored your pleas?

5. What flashes through your mind when Jesus started the riddle? Why did you answer Jesus as you did?

6. What kind of feelings do you have when Jesus finally responds positively?

7. What do you think Jesus learned from this experience?

8. Do you feel more powerful after the encounter with Jesus?

Discuss each meditation question with the group and share responses. You may end the meditation time with prayer or with a simple "Amen."

Spiritual Exercise II: Who Are the Saints?

The purpose of this exercise is to rediscover the original intention of the term "saint." The leader may wish to have at hand some of the resources listed under Further Reading for the group members to explore.

On a blank piece of paper, each member should draw a line down the middle and then write down the following headings.

Type (A) Saint
List the characteristics you held of a "saint" before you began this study. What are attributes traditionally thought of as saintly?

Type (B) Saint
List the characteristics of a "saint" as described in the first two chapters of this book.

After the members have decided upon their list of characteristics, the leader should help the group draw up a composite description of Type A Saint and Type B Saint. This means that the characteristics on each member's list will be combined to form one single definition. The leader can help the process by recalling key ideas from the chapters, for example, the content of footnote 2 and 3 in Chapter 2. Post the descriptions of Saint A and Saint B on two sheets of newsprint.

When the group has agreed on a composite description, the leader may choose from among several activities.

1. Discuss what persons in the Bible fit either type Saint A or Saint B. Give the reasons for your selections.
2. Volunteers may choose to act out or role play their vision of what each type of saint might be like.
3. The group might tell stories of people *they know* who fit both saintly categories.
4. End with prayer:

Almighty God, by your Holy Spirit you have made us one with your saints in heaven and on earth: Grant that in our earthly pilgrimage we may always be supported by this fellowship of love and prayer, and know ourselves to be surrounded by their witness to your power and mercy. We ask this for the sake of Jesus Christ, in whom all our intercessions are acceptable. Amen.[19]

Spiritual Exercise III

If the group wishes to try another spiritual exercise you might choose Exercise 6, "Toward Wholeness and Health," in Carolyn Stahl, *Opening to God,* pp. 63-64.

---

[19] *The Book of Common Prayer* (New York: The Church Hymnal Corporation and The Seabury Press, 1977), p. 250.

Further Readings

I am often asked for resources that provide material about the faith stories of Christians in other eras. The best place to begin is with a few good dictionaries of the saints. The two I use most often are: John J. Delaney, *Dictionary of Saints* (Garden City, New York: Doubleday & Company, Inc., 1980) and, David Hugh Farmer, *The Oxford Dictionary of Saints* (Oxford: Clarendon Press, 1978). If you are in range of a theological library, it is always fun to read the 18th-century perspective on saints in Alban Butler's four volume *Lives of the Saints*. A concise 1985 paperback edition of Butler's work, called *Butler's Lives of the Saints*, is edited by Michael Walsh and published in England by Burns & Oates, Wellwood, North Farm Road, Turnbridge Wells, Kent TN2 3 DR. The paperback second edition of *The Penguin Dictionary of Saints*, edited by Donald Attwater and published by Penguin books is reliable but gives only abridged details. Short biographical sketches of seventy "saints" may be found in Elliott Wright, *Holy Company, Christian Heroes and Heroines* (New York: Macmillan Publishing Co., Inc., 1980).

Lawrence Cunningham's book *The Meaning of Saints* (San Francisco: Harper & Row, 1980) provides an important interpretation of sanctity for the life of the Church. *The Saint Book, for Parents, Teachers, Homilists, Storytellers and Children* by Mary Reed Newland (New York: Seabury Press, 1979) is a wonderful resource. Finally, the splendid series of small paperback books for children, published by Winston Press (Minneapolis, Minnesota, 1977), entitled *Stories about Christian Heroes*, includes the lives of contemporary people as well as historical figures. Other publishing houses that have interesting childrens' books on saints are Augsburg Publishing House, Concordia Press and Seabury Press.

Additional Resource

Diedra Kriewald, "Called To Be The Saints," (a sermon taped at *Proclamation*, a National Conference on Preaching, 1984). Order from *The United Methodist Lecture Series*, P. O. Box 801, Nashville, Tennessee, 37202. (Single tapes $5.60).

PART II

THREE PROBLEMS: OPPRESSION, HUNGER, POWERLESSNESS

CHAPTER III

DEVOURING FIRE

The glory of the Lord looked to the Israelites like a devouring fire on the mountain top.
(Exodus 24:17, NEB)

Students from Wesley Theological Seminary were taking a guided walk through an area of Washington, D.C. which is particularly rich in international flavor. In a section of the city whose characteristics are dominated by the activities of recent immigrants, the students were astonished as our escort stopped before a series of ordinary buildings and announced that these apartments were inhabited by a complete village from El Salvador. How had the citizens of this village arrived in our nation's capital? The whole village, led by their priest, had walked (yes, walked!) all the way from El Salvador to the United States border. Why had they left? They walked out of their homeland because of the indiscriminate violence that had killed many members of their village. Were they in this country legally? Yes and no. But they were willing to risk the hazards of refugee status to escape from *oppression*.

The suffering caused by oppression is difficult to analyze objectively. We know that this type of suffering happens every day in our world. It is not always easy, however, to pin down who is responsible for the suffering. The issues are often clouded by the political rivalries of competing groups and our own devotion to national self-interest. Statistics from remote parts of the globe are hard to translate into individual persons. Sometimes it is not clear what is meant by the words "oppressors" or "victims."

It may help us to consider the following definitions. These descriptions are compiled from the work of several biblical scholars who write from the "down under" perspective of Christians living in developing countries.[1] The scripture quotations relate to images of oppression.

Oppression

Oppression describes an experience in which persons with power, for their own gain, take unfair advantage of their position to abuse those less powerful. Basic human rights are denied. Oppression is experienced as a dehumanizing state causing anxiety and fear (Isaiah 59:9-15). In the Bible, the experience of oppression is closely connected with the antagonism that exists between the rich and poor (I Kings 21); but oppression can be the result of racial, sexual, religious or political ideas which are used by the powerful to exploit the weaker (Zechariah 7:8-12; Isaiah 3:12-15).

Oppressors

By definition, oppressors have the power to force their social, economic or political will on others who do not have an effective means of resisting. The Old Testament acknowledges two different kinds of oppressors: stronger nations who press their national interests on weaker nations (Jeremiah 30:8-9; Isaiah 19:20) and leaders holding power within a nation who establish and enforce unjust laws and customs (Ezekiel 22:17-31).[2]

Oppressors have power because they have greater wealth than their victims and they are usually allied with the governing classes. The most common objective of those

---

[1] See theological word studies in works by José Míguez Bonino, Gustavo Gutiérrez, Tomás Hanks and Elsa Tamez. Books by these authors are published by the Catholic Foreign Mission Society of America (Maryknoll) through Orbis Books, Maryknoll, New York 10545.

[2] Elsa Tamez, *Bible of the Oppressed* (Maryknoll, New York: Orbis Books, 1982), pp. 32-33.

who oppress others is to maintain or increase their own wealth and influence and to preserve a privileged way of life (Amos 2:6-7; 5:21-24; 6:1-7).[3]

Who Are the Oppressors?

Oppressors come in all shapes, sizes, and both sexes (remember Amos' colorful description of the greedy wives as the "cows of Bashan"!—Amos 4:1); all races, economic classes and nationalities have been oppressors. They might be government officials, military leaders, business corporations, religious organizations, judges or just ordinary individuals within any society who use their personal power to violate, exploit or degrade their weaker neighbors (Amos 5:7-15; Hosea 12:6-9; Jeremiah 22:13-17).

Oppressors may use ruthless violence to maintain their power. Or oppressors may appear personally generous and benevolent while cherishing and upholding a legal and social system which allows them to play a patronizing and condescending role to those who are kept in political and economic servitude (Micah 2:1-2).

The Oppressed

The characteristics of the oppressed are the opposite of those who have power. They are the powerless people, with no social standing and little money or prestige to help themselves change their lives. The poor are needy and easily oppressed. Often uneducated and undertrained, the poor are oppressed *because they are poor* and have no means of resistance. They are also *poor because they are oppressed.*[4]

Traditionally the elderly, aliens or refugees in the land, persons with disabilities, women of all ages and children have been easy victims of oppressors because prevailing social structures have not allowed these groups the accumulated means of power to fight back (Isaiah 10:1-3; Ezekiel 22:29-30).

---

[3] It should be noted that it is not wealth itself that the Bible condemns but the use of that wealth to dominate and control the lives of others.

[4] Elsa Tamez, *Bible of the Oppressed*, p. 37.

Oppression: A Continuing Human Problem

In the world today there are powerful persons who take unfair advantage of their position to abuse those less powerful. In South Africa, Nobel Peace Prize winner in 1984, Anglican Bishop Desmond Tutu, strongly asserts that despite some cosmetic improvements, apartheid cannot be liberalized because "you can't improve something that is intrinsically evil."[5] Oppression is the way of life for the black people who make up the majority of the population in South Africa.[6]

Dateline: *The Washington Post*—1 May 1985: International relief workers at Ibnet, a highland feeding camp in Ethiopia, report that government soldiers ordered 60,000 famine victims out of the camp and told them to walk back from where they came. The soldiers then burned the grass huts that had been occupied by the refugees. **Update:** *The Washington Post*—9 May 1985: After an international cry of outrage at the military action at Ibnet, the government of Ethiopia announced that the famine victims could walk back to the camp. As the hungry returned, the few relief workers were overwhelmed; all living quarters had been burned, new latrines would have to be dug, and the fear of disease hung in the air just as surely as did the smell of starvation. Oppression of the weak and hopeless is real in Ethiopia.

The tragedy taking place in South Africa and in Ethiopia is only a sampler—there are three million Afghan refugees in Pakistan fleeing from oppression. Millions more Biafrans, Palestinians, Yemenites, South Sudanese, Ugandans, Khurds and Cambodians have been massacred in recent years. *Amnesty International* reported in 1985 that torture is on the increase throughout the world. Daily there are news reports of violence in the Philippines and in Central America.

This oppression is not happening in some uncivilized

---

[5] "Dealing with Apartheid," *Newsweek*, March 11, 1985, p. 32.

[6] Desmond Tutu, *Hope and Suffering* (Grand Rapids, Michigan: William B. Eerdmans Publishing Company, 1984) is a good introduction to the religious perspective of this great Christian leader.

world a thousand years ago—this misery is happening NOW! The common thread in all these cases is the unjustified suffering of innocent people caused by the deliberate actions of more powerful others. Included in these statistics are individuals just like you or me. They are living persons caught in the deadly trap of political and economic tyranny.

There is much to ponder in this data. Before we get bogged down in statistics and definitions, perhaps we should change direction and participate in a spiritual exercise that may help us to assimilate the meaning of oppression. You may do this exercise now or wait until the end of the study session.

CLUSTERING

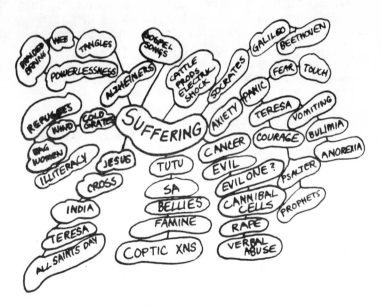

You are looking at a technique called "clustering." Clustering is free association around a central word. The clustering of ideas around this central image is a window into your mind, believes Gabriele Lusser Rico, who designed the cluster system as a creative technique for natural writing.[7]

Examine the cluster diagram at the start of the spiritual exercise. The central nuclear word around which this cluster is built is the word "suffering." This particular cluster of words is the result of my own brainstorming effort in order to get started with ideas for this book. You will recognize in this cluster many of the issues that are discussed in these pages.

Why don't you try the clustering exercise by freely associating around the theme of oppression? Here is the way to begin:

1. *Prayer:* Begin with prayer. Sit quietly and take a few slow, deep breaths. Ask God to help you think clearly on the subject of the suffering caused by oppression.

2. *The Nucleus:* Clustering is begun by circling a single "nuclear" word on a clean page of paper. Write the word "oppression" in the middle of your page and then circle it. Then while sitting quietly, let the ideas and images begin to flow.

3. *Clustering the Ideas:* Words, images, and experiences will begin to come to your mind around the word "oppression." You may remember scenes from television news, from newspaper or magazine reports and from your own life experiences. The designer of the exercise says simply to "let go" and begin to "write down rapidly" the flow of the connections that come into your head.

Write the words, each idea in its own circle, radiating outward from the center word in any direction they seem to want to go. Then connect each new word with a line to another circled word on the page. When you exhaust that stream of consciousness, begin again with a new idea from the central nucleus and radiate outward as before.

4. *Share:* Share some of your clusters with the study group. It is not necessary to explain everything you have written down. Some of your associations about the suffering caused by oppression may be painful and not easily shared. You can also use initials or your own code words for those ideas you may wish to keep private. However, do share at least one of your associations with the group.

---

[7] Gabriele Lusser Rico, *Writing the Natural Way* (Boston: Houghton Mifflin Company, 1983), chapter 2.

The Courage of Contemporary Martyrs

There is not a Christian reading this book who does not know that the early church was persecuted by the Roman empire. To be sure, the persecutions were intermittent, localized and certainly not uniform throughout the empire. Dreadful times of persecution, however, did result in the deaths of many Christians. The early Christian communities kept records of these deaths. As early as the second century, the church publically venerated the martyrs. The word "martyr" means "witness," and regular liturgical commemorations beginning in the second century marked anniversaries of the deaths of those who gave the ultimate witness for Christ.

The recognition that there are still Christian martyrs became a reality for me during the week of 24 March 1980 when Oscar Arnulfo Romero, the sixty-three-year-old Roman Catholic archbishop of San Salvador was gunned down while saying Mass in the chapel of a hospital that he had helped build for dying cancer victims. In his last public sermon, Archbishop Romero had thundered, "I ask you, I pray you, I order you in the name of God, stop the repression." Six of the priests under his charge had been violently killed that year. The response of somebody was to stop Romero. He followed Jesus too well into Jerusalem that 1980 Holy Week—right past the hosannas and into the Temple. The archbishop took too many stands, upset too many tables and preached too many dangerous sermons on the subject of political and economic reform.

The dramatic setting for Romero's assassination at the very moment he was celebrating Holy Communion lent a feeling of unreality to his death. I had just seen a rerun of the movie "Becket" on television. I had the eerie feeling that Archbishop Romero belonged on the screen with Richard Burton—so far removed was I from the terror in the everyday lives of a large majority of my Central American neighbors. The events in San Salvador were as bloodily real, however, as was the twelfth century assassination of Thomas à Becket for his religious convictions by the henchmen of Henry II.

The names of Benigno Aquino, who was assassinated in the Philippines, and Martin Luther King, Jr., who was murdered in the United States are recorded along with that of Oscar Romero in the book of the martyrs, as surely as those unnamed Christian heroes heralded in Revelation 6:9. Included in the continuing roll of the martyrs are four Catholic laywomen from the United States who were also murdered in El Salvador and two troublesome nuns who, with concrete tied around their necks, were dropped to their death from an airplane by members of the Argentinean military before the Falklands war. After the war, it was revealed that the murderers referred to their victims as "the flying nuns."[8]

Since 1983, I have kept an informal count of new martyrs. Each time I read of another death, I mentally record the situation and say prayers for that person by name at the next worship service I lead or attend. In the newspaper delivered to my door this morning on 14 May 1985, there was a world news item that told of four Soviet Pentecostal Christians seeking to emigrate to the West who tried to force their way into the U.S. Embassy. Three of the Christians were beaten and arrested by uniformed Soviet guards at the embassy door. The fourth Pentecostalist managed to slip inside during the melee. U.S. embassy officers interviewed the man for two hours and then told him he had to leave. U.S. officials drove him in a diplomatic vehicle to a Moscow subway station. The man was arrested before he could enter the station and was taken away in a Soviet police car. I do not know the names of these Pentecostal brothers. Our theological positions are probably quite different. Nevertheless my day began with a silent prayer for their survival.

During this academic year, I have said public prayers for: United Methodist missionary-pilot Stanley G. Ridgway who was shot and killed on November 13 in Zaire; two Pentecostal Holiness educators who are missing and presumed dead in Guatemala; Brother André, a French missionary-priest in Chile who was shot to death while he said private evening prayers in his room (just after he had tried to stop violence

---

[8] "Volubly Silent," *The Christian Century*, May 15, 1985, p. 490. See also Thomas S. Goslin "Argentina's *Desaparecidos:* Investigating Their Fate, *The Christian Century*, April 17, 1985, pp. 382-383.

between police and students); and for Jerzy Popieluiszko, the popular Polish priest who was beaten and then drowned by high ranking officials for his pro-Solidarity labor activities.

These five Christians are well-known because of their vocational connection to church bodies. The countless laypersons endangered for reasons of faith, as in South Africa, are not so easily identifiable. It must also be clearly understood that the Church is called to pray for all oppressed people regardless of their religious affiliation. Courage is a human trait and not the private preserve of any one religion.

In spite of the danger, courage abounds in a world filled with oppression. Of the many stories that should be told and retold in our churches, here are two stories of bravery that exemplify victorious nonviolent resistance to oppression by the Christian laity.

Christ in a Poncho: Adolfo Pérez Esquivel and the Mothers of the Plaza de Mayo[9]

The terrorism began in 1976 after a military coup when teenagers and young college students began to disappear in Argentina. Since these missing youth had been agitating for political freedom and social reform, it was assumed that they were being kidnapped by security forces. In the seven years between 1976 and 1983 thousands of children, youth and young adults (some estimates are as high as 15,000) disappeared from Argentinean society without a trace, with no records or few clues as to their fate. They are called *los Desaparecidos*—the disappeared.

In this climate of fear, a number of mothers of the missing youth began to meet to encourage one another and to overcome their despair. One Thursday a group of these mothers held a silent demonstration in the Plaza de Mayo, which is the square right in the center of Buenos Aires and opposite the federal buildings. The next step was a candlelight vigil. The official response was predictably violent. The mothers were hosed, gassed, and arrested, and

---

[9] Material for this story is from Charles Antoine, editor, *Christ in a Poncho, Testimonials of the Nonviolent Struggles in Latin America* (Maryknoll, New York: Orbis Books, 1983).

51

some disappeared along with their missing children. The women continued to hold weekly marches for several years silently holding up names or photographs with the words, "Where is my child?" The police called them the "mad-women of the Plaza de Mayo."[10]

The mothers sought out the support of an international organization called The Peace and Justice Service, a Christian organization committed to working for nonviolent change while promoting peace, justice and human rights. The Latin American coordinator for Peace and Justice Service was Adolfo Pérez Esquivel. It was Adolfo Pérez Esquivel that organized the continual nonviolent protests of the "mothers" but not before he paid dearly for this activity at the hands of the Argentinean system of justice.

Adolfo Pérez Esquivel was an unlikely hero—now about fifty-five, a painter and sculptor-teacher by profession, married to Amanda Esquivel, a pianist and composer. When Pérez Esquivel was forty years old, he became interested in the nonviolent liberation movements fer-menting in Latin America and began to travel out of the country to visit Christian communities in other countries who were working for human rights.

On one of these trips to Ecuador, Adolfo Esquivel dreamed one night that he saw Christ on the cross wearing an Indian poncho, the dress of the poor. A few days later, he went into a small chapel and stood riveted before an unusual crucifix. Jesus was there on the wall, Christ crucified, in a poncho just as he had appeared in Adolfo's dream. "From then on," Pérez Esquivel says, "he [the Christ in the poncho] never let me alone." He felt an urgent call to serve as an advocate for the poor, the missing, the prisoners and all those who were marginalized and exploited in Argentina.

Arrested as soon as he returned from Ecuador, Adolfo was held for over two years without indictment. In La Plata Prison he was forbidden all books, even a Bible. The

---

[10] For another true story of Christian women who battled an oppressive government in La Paz, Bolivia at Christmastime, 1977 see Esther and Mortimer Arias, *The Cry of My People* (New York: Friendship Press, 1980), pp. 90-92.

captivity started with thirty-two days in what was called "the Pipe"—so named because it was a very narrow, L-shaped cell just long enough for a prisoner to lie down, with just a little space at the door to stand up. He was beaten and tortured. They tried to get him to insult God and the reformist bishops that he knew. He declares that "it was prayer that was my mainstay in prison." Faced with long days and nights of solitude, he came to appreciate what he called "God's silence." "Here everything is taken," he wrote, "we are naked before God, with our fears, our questions, our pain—but in all confidence in God's grace."

Fourteen more months of house arrest followed his release from prison. If the government intended to intimidate him, the tactic did not work. When the ban was lifted, Adolfo Pérez Esquivel immediately took up the work right where he had left off. In July, 1980, he organized the Mothers of the Plaza de Mayo into a major political force whose protest would be heard around the world.

By the estimates of his co-workers, Adolfo Pérez Esquivel is not a very charismatic figure. He has skills in coordinating and organizing, but he is not a great speaker. At one time he wrote, "True, the elephant is stronger. But the ants—well, there are more of them." Adolfo sees himself as an ant organizing other ants in the vision of the Christ-sign, the Christ who wears the poncho, the Christ of the poor.

On 13 October 1980, it was announced that the Nobel Peace Prize had been awarded to Adolfo Pérez Esquivel. One Argentinean radio station reporting the story said that he was a Brazilian. Another Argentine reporter hypothesized that he was from Paraguay. The unknown, unnamed courageous mothers who persisted year after year in their silent vigil at the Plaza del Mayo knew his identity. As this book is being written, several leading military officers are on trial for terrorist activities during this period.

Baptism by Fire: Fannie Lou Hamer[11]

The stories we tell in The United States of America about

---

[11] Material for the story of Fannie Lou Hamer comes from Pam McAllister, editor, *Reweaving the Web of Life, Feminism and Nonviolence* (Philadelphia: New Society Publishers, 1982), pp. 106-111.

the founding of this country have to do with freedom from oppression. Proudly we recall Puritans and Pilgrims, Quakers and debtors who fled from the old European world to establish a new life of freedom. Unfortunately, the concept of "freedom" has sometimes been reserved for the look-alike cultural relatives of this European majority. Fortunately North Americans have had strong prophetic voices from within and without the religious communities who have called this country to a more just future. Fannie Lou Hamer was one of those prophetic voices.

In the summer of 1962, the same summer that my husband and the three youths were killed on a Mexican highway, Fannie Lou Hamer and seventeen other poor and black sharecroppers signed up to go to the Sunflower County Courthouse in Indianola, Mississippi, in order to make the attempt to register to vote. She was quite simply a poor woman who was lured by the magic word "freedom." All eighteen failed the registration test that day, but Mrs. Hamer made up her mind that she would come back again and again until she became a "first class citizen."

The same day of the twenty-six mile bus trip to the courthouse, Fannie Lou Hamer was fired from the plantation where she had worked as a sharecropper for eighteen years. Her husband, who had worked there for thirty years, was also fired and their car and furniture confiscated by the plantation owner.

With no place to go, no money and no possibility of a job, the Hamers became virtual fugitives. Moving from friend to friend, they were constantly pursued by cars full of white men armed with rifles, who rode back and forth in front of the houses, shouting obscenities and threatening to shoot.

The abuse seemed only to stiffen her resolve and she went back to the Sunflower County Courthouse every thirty days until she finally passed the examination on 10 January 1963. Fanny Lou Hamer began working to recruit other blacks to register. Five months later, she paid heavily for the right to be a citizen.

On the way to a voter education workshop in Charleston, South Carolina, Fanny Lou Hamer and some of the group were arrested as they got off at a rest stop to use the washroom. At the local jail they were interrogated. These are her own words which were recorded in The Congressional Record of 16 June 1964:

> They said they were going to make me wish I was dead. They had me lay down on my face, and they ordered two Negro prisoners to beat me with a blackjack. That was unbearable. It was leather, loaded with something.
>
> The first prisoner beat me until he was exhausted. Then the second Negro began to beat. . . .
>
> I began to move my feet. The State Highway patrolman ordered the other Negro to sit on my feet. My dress pulled up and I tried to smooth it down. One of the policemen walked over and raised my dress as high as he could. They beat me until my body was hard, 'till I couldn't bend my fingers or get up when they told me to. That's how I got this blood clot on my left eye—the sight's nearly gone, now. And my kidney was injured from the blows they gave me in the back.

After the beating, she was thrown into a cell, battered and bloody, where she listened to the screams of Ann Ponder, who was being beaten in another cell. She told the members of the United States Congress that she heard her torturers "plotting to kill us, maybe to throw our bodies in the Big Black River, where nobody would ever find us." Andrew Young and James Bevel came to the jail and carried her out only half conscious.

As soon as she was able to walk, Fannie Lou Hamer was out in the cotton fields, limping and nauseated with pain, trying to line up prospective voters. She spent her evenings going from church to church in the countryside talking about voter registration and singing the spiritual songs of freedom.

Because of the courageous witness of black citizens like Fannie Lou Hamer, our country was forced to stop oppressing many of its citizens. Mrs. Hamer continued to help those in need and opened a Day Care Center for the children of low-income and working parents. In 1970 she announced the success of Freedom Farm Co-operative, which, in that year, had fed 1,500 people, both blacks and whites from forty acres.

The Righteous Fire of God

Images help us to examine a difficult topic when statistics seem too cold or remote and faith stories seem too close and painful. The biblical image of "fire" as it relates to the suffering caused by oppression may help explain the Christian mission.

In the biblical world, fire was a symbol of the divine presence. The voice of the "I AM" called Moses in the flames of a burning bush that was never consumed (Exodus 2:3). A strange pillar of fire gave light to the people of the Exodus as they made their way from Egypt. In one climactic moment, Moses brought the Hebrew refugees to meet God at the foot of Mount Sinai. The people were terrified for, as scripture records, the Lord came down upon the sacred mountain like fire (Exodus 19:18).

The justice of God is often symbolized in the Old Testament by the image of fire. Abraham J. Heschel, in his monumental study of the prophets, asserts that there are few thoughts as deeply ingrained in biblical thought as the fact of God's righteousness.[12] Gathered together by Ezekiel in one powerful passage is a catalog of the abuses of civic and religious responsibility of those who lived in Jerusalem just before its destruction in 587 B.C. Ezekiel's description could fit any number of nations in the world today: (1) the leaders are like lions devouring the people, taking all the money and property they can get, and by their murders leaving many widows; (2) the priests break the law and have no respect for what is holy; (3) the military officers are like wolves tearing their prey and shedding blood to get rich; (4) the prophets cover up these sins like whitewash; (5) the common people cheat and rob; they mistreat the poor and are also unjust and cruel to foreigners (Ezekiel 22:17-31).

The reaction of God to this situation was angry and decisive. The Israelites were useless like waste metal. Thus they would be gathered into a crucible and the rage of the Lord would melt them the way fire melts ore (Ezekiel 22:20-22). Well, now! The word of the Lord could not be clearer. Fire is a very strong sign indeed pointing beyond itself to the divine power—a righteous power that calls the people of God to establish a world built on justice. Seek

---

[12] Abraham J. Heschel, *The Prophets* (New York: Harper & Row, 1962), pp. 199-200.

justice, correct oppression, defend the fatherless and plead for the widow is the vision of Isaiah (Isaiah 1:17).

Jesus makes an equally strong statement declaring that for those who cause a child or a "little one" to stumble, it would be better if a millstone were hung around their necks and they were drowned. Jesus concludes, "Alas for the world that such causes of stumbling arise! Come they must, but woe betide the one through whom they come!" (Matthew 18:6-7, NEB).

The "little ones" referred to by Jesus has a wider meaning than *children*. "Little ones" is a term for his humble, rank-and-file followers. Jesus is expressing concern here for those powerless and vulnerable adults who are childlike in their helplessness. The spirit of the scripture is captured by Lynne Locke in a poem entitled "A Divine Fierceness."

"Don't bar the little ones,"
growls the fierce Jesus.
They sit inside his paws
and watch the people
fade away at promise
of millstones and deep seas.

So mild he was, saying,
"They know not what they do."
But that was for himself.
For the children he says,
"Harm these little ones
and I will eat you alive
and spit out your bones."
They are so safe sitting inside
the growls of their fierce Jesus.[13]

On the Jewish festival of Pentecost, the Spirit Advocate came to a gathering of the followers of the risen Christ bringing "tongues, like flames of fire." From that day on, Christians join in the fire of the Holy Spirit to work for the realization of the reign of God. Those who accept this ministry are also promised the inner resources, by the grace of God, to face the tough prospect of making justice a living reality in this world (Jeremiah 20:7-13). The exaltation of promised victory is captured in the words of Zephania

---

[13] Lynn Locke, "A Divine Fierceness," *Alive Now!* (Nashville: The Upper Room, July/August 1985), p. 44. Used by permission.

Kameeta of Namibia, Africa:

> As smoke is blown away
> and wax melts in the fire,
> racism and oppression
> disappear before the face of God.
> The oppressed and trampled down
> are set free in God's presence.
> They rejoice and shout with joy.[14]

We can be certain that God is present and active wherever there is suffering caused by oppression. Comfortable Christians ignore the biblical message at great spiritual peril. Martyrs do not die because torture makes them feel saintly or because they like doing good works. Action against oppression is the natural result of believing in a righteous God. Justice is required by a just God. Because Christians accept the biblical belief in a God whose very character is righteousness and whose mode of action is justice, *therefore* Christians are compelled to engage in social action.[15] But there is a cost. Author Flannery O'Conner speaks "the gospel truth" when she writes:

> What people don't realize is how much religion costs. They think faith is a big electric blanket, when of course, it is the cross.[16]

One cross to bear is the fact that our best efforts are not always effective. It is hard to remember as injustice persists that we are called continually to care for the neighbor. The Psalmist laments for all of us that the wicked seem to prosper and amass great wealth (Psalm 73). By the world's standard, Jesus was ineffective. Nevertheless, Christians conclude: "what we are offered in Christ is a story that helps us sustain the task of charity in a world where it can never

---

[14] Zephania Kameeta, "As Smoke Is Blown Away," *No Longer Strangers*, edit. by Iben Gjerding and Katherine Kinnamon (Geneva: W.C.C. Publications, 1984), p. 39.

[15] "In short, it is not enough to say that God is the one who saves and blesses in these stories; what is crucial is *the kind of* God who is understood to be saving and blessing." Terrence E. Fretheim, *The Suffering of God, An Old Testament Perspective* in *Overtures to Biblical Theology* (Philadelphia: Fortress Press, 1984), p. 24.

[16] Flannery O'Conner, *The Habit of Being* (New York: Farrar, Straus, & Giroux, 1979), p. 354.

be successful."[17] Mother Teresa continues to pick up the dying off the streets of Calcutta, even though she knows there will be hundreds more. She has "such a vision of the street as the street hardly knows." When asked why she continues the work in spite of such small success, she replies that it is "something beautiful for God."[18]

Grab a Lifeline[19]

Make no mistake! Christians who live in secure circumstances are also under the mandate of the just God to eliminate oppression in their own communities. And those of us on safer shores are called to become a link in the lifeline of the human neighborhood. Technically a lifeline is defined as: (1) a rope for saving life—as one thrown to a person in the deep water; (2) any rope fastened where it may be clutched by persons in danger by being swept away and drowned; (3) a route that is safe where information and supplies can be transported to a certain place.

The suffering caused by oppression is a very complex and overwhelming phenomenon; nevertheless, becoming a member of the human lifeline requires only some first simple steps:

First—Overcome Indifference

Christians who are lucky enough to live in an environment of freedom may need to overcome their indifference to oppression. In remarks on the occasion of accepting a Congressional Gold Medal in May, 1985, Elie Wiesel, survivor of the Holocaust, declared, "The greatest evil is indifference."[20] Abraham Heschel believes that "Indifference to evil is more insidious than evil itself; it is more universal, more contagious, more dangerous."[21] Many of us are so secure, comfortable and preoccupied with everyday matters that we are not even aware of what is happening to

[17] Hauerwas, *Truthfulness and Tragedy*, pp. 133-138.
[18] Eileen Egan, *Such a Vision of the Street* (Garden City, New York: Doubleday & Company, 1985), p. 72.
[19] The lifeline image comes from the lead song by Holly Near and Ronnie Gilbert in their album, *Lifeline*.
[20] Quoted in *The Washington Post*, April 20, 1985.
[21] Abraham Heschel, *The Prophets*, p. 284.

our sisters and brothers right here in this country much less around the world. Overcoming indifference involves a commitment to be concerned about the suffering of oppression no matter how far removed it seems from our own lives or how hopeless the situation appears to be.

Second—Become a Global Christian

North American church people need to think of themselves as global Christians. The Church rallies to international need when there is a major crisis, such as in the continuing famine in Africa. Most of us, however, are not used to thinking of our faith in ecumenical and international terms. It may be natural to expend our religious energies within our own denominations and in the setting of our local congregations, but when the Church reflects on oppression, it must consider the needs and concerns of *all*, regardless of faith family or area of the world. Corrupt landholders neither politely inquire as to the denominational affiliation of impoverished peasants, nor do death squads ask their victims the same question.

An important deepening of our spiritual lives will begin when we teach ourselves to search for information about the church universal. When you read the daily newspaper or a weekly newsmagazine, watch for reports of endangered churches throughout the world. Read journals of Christian opinion that carry international items. Share information within your congregation. You might want to start a bulletin board with news from around the world.

Third—Develop a Lifeline of Prayer

Prayer is one kind of Christian lifeline that binds all together across the stormy waves. At the very least, all Christians can uphold each other before God. The corporate prayer life of a congregation reflects the real values and concerns of the church. How many prayers in the worship services that you have attended lately have been for those outside the immediate concern of your congregation? Is your parish aware of the number of Christian martyrs in this world? Perhaps your group could ask those responsible for the Sunday liturgy to include a prayer each week for the Church in a different troubled area. Don't forget to pray for non-Christians who are also members of the human family.

Fourth—Tell the Stories of Courage

We must tell the stories of faith. In a very particular way today, God seems to be speaking to those of us who are secure through the courage of those who live under oppressive circumstances. Christians who live in dangerous circumstances are the ones who can tell us (as in the days of the early Church) what it is like to live fully the gospel. We listen to their stories with gratitude and humility and marvel at God's grace.

Fifth—Work with the Structures Already in Place

Become aware of the work already being done for peace and justice by various boards and agencies within the denomination. You may find a way to have an effective voice through already existing structures. Don't be afraid to become involved in political activity. Join with other churches to work for a more equitable and just community life.

Sometimes we overlook oppressive structures in our own churches and neighborhoods. Persons with various disabling conditions are often unfairly labeled as a burden to family and society. The decision makers and power holders in every town and in each congregation decide whether to spend or withhold the funds to make buildings architecturally accessible to persons with movement disabilities. Every congregation has hearing impaired persons; in fact, all of us stand a chance of becoming hearing impaired as we grow older. What steps has your congregation taken to insure that those members with sight or hearing loss will feel at home in the liturgy? Can persons with mental retardation be genuinely included in your congregation? Oppression is experienced as a dehumanizing state which causes anxiety and fear. Does your ministry foster freedom for those with disabling conditions?[22]

---

[22] There is an excellent study book from the Task Force of Persons with Disabilities, Gerald F. Moede, *God's Power and Our Weakness* (Princeton, New Jersey: Consultation on Church Union). Copies are available from Consultation on Church Union, 228 Alexander Street, Princeton, New Jersey 08540. Also see Jean Vanier, *The Challenge of l'Arche* (Minneapolis: Winston Press, 1981), for the inspirational story of home ministries to persons with severe handicapping conditions.

The old gospel song, "Throw Out The Lifeline," takes on new meaning in light of the suffering caused by oppression. We need to sing its message often.

Throw out the lifeline across the dark wave!
There is a neighbor whom someone should save;
Somebody's neighbor! Oh who then will dare,
To throw out the lifeline, the peril to share?

Throw out the lifeline! Throw out the lifeline!
Someone is drifting away; Throw out the lifeline!
Throw out the lifeline! Someone is sinking today.[23]

Questions for Discussion

1. Have you ever been oppressed by government authorities or by persons holding power? Do you know individuals who have suffered great oppression? Review the definition of the "Oppressed" given earlier in the chapter. Share stories of courage from your own experiences or from those of your friends and family.

2. Have you ever been an oppressor? Were you aware that you were unjustly exercising power? Has anyone in your family been an overt oppressor? How did you feel about the experience? Why do you think persons become oppressors?

3. Do you agree that God's righteousness is like a "devouring fire"? What truth does this biblical metaphor convey? Is there a "divine fierceness" for justice? Do we talk openly of God's judgment in today's churches? Or do we often act, as Flannery O'Connor suggests, as if faith is a big electric blanket?

4. Read again the definition of a "lifeline." A safe route is one kind of lifeline. Harriet Tubman led this kind of lifeline through the Underground Railroad (a network of secret places that helped slaves escape to the North during the Civil War). Is the Christian Sanctuary movement another lifeline, providing safe routes to freedom for Latin American refugees?

---

[23] Edward S. Ufford, *Songs of Zion* (Nashville: Abingdon, 1981), p. 56.

Spiritual Exercises

Exercise 1: You may now want to participate in the clustering exercise found at the beginning of this chapter unless the group has done so earlier.

Exercise 2: This exercise is a variation of a model used by Norman E. Leach to sensitize a high school class on the subject of labeling persons with handicapping conditions.[24]

1. Write these words on newsprint or a blackboard: NIGGER, WOP, KIKE, SPIC, QUEER, YHWH, CHRIST-KILLER, OLD, ELDERLY, FAT, OBESE, REDNECK, DEAF AND DUMB, A-RAB, CRIPPLE, RETARDED, FOREIGNER.

2. Ask the group what each word means (except the letters YHWH). How does each word define the person? These words are *not* names of people, but we use them as if they were names. Actually, the words are *labels* which are used to define people.

3. Do these words have the power to define an individual's humanity by the meaning understood in the label? Can you give an example from your own experience of being defined by a label?

4. How do we use such words to control and oppress others? Can you think of examples where such labeling leads to political or economic oppression?

5. Discuss the letters YHWH and ask what they represent. YHWH (Yahweh) is the Hebrew name for God. But, after the Exile, the Hebrews did not speak the name of God, YHWH, for that would be to have put a restriction on God. Thus the word, *adonai*, the LORD, was spoken instead, and the letters, YHWH, only represented God on the symbolic level. God is the one who is called the "I AM" (Exodus 3:13-14). How is this label different from the ones we ordinarily give people?

6. How can we help persons obtain the right to define their own lives? What is the Christian responsibility to overcome the labeling that leads to oppression?

7. Close the discussion with prayer.

---

[24] This exercise is found in *God's Power and Our Weakness*, edited by Gerald F. Moede, pp. 3-5.

63

Exercise 3: A nonsectarian project that might interest your study group is the letter writing campaign against oppression by Amnesty International. Amnesty International is a highly respected grassroots organization that monitors human rights in the world. Amnesty was awarded the Nobel Peace Prize in 1977 and "enjoys a reputation for scrupulous research and strict impartiality as it catalogs abuses and uses its membership to pressure offending governments."[25]

The membership of Amnesty is broken down into small "adoption" groups which are formed in churches and synagogues, clubs, offices or any small group of people who care about human rights. Each group is assigned two "prisoners of conscience" who have been incarcerated solely for their religious or political beliefs or for their ethnic origins. To be helped by Amnesty, the prisoner must have neither used nor advocated violence.

Basically, the adoption group follows the fate of the prisoners of conscience assigned to them. They send letters of encouragement to the victims and carefully worded appeals for freedom to anyone who might be able to influence the prisoner's release. Amnesty also makes a general appeal to its membership for letters in emergency situations. Amnesty's letter-writing campaigns are often very effective.

Amnesty International is a "lifeline" of women and men who are committed to doing something specific about the suffering caused by oppression. If your study group wishes more information, write to: Amnesty International USA, 322 Eighth Avenue, New York, New York 10001.

---

[25] Michael Satchell, "Political Prisoners, The Forgotten People," *Parade Magazine*, May 12, 1985, p. 5.

Further Reading

Arias, Esther and Mortimer. *The Cry of My People, Out of Captivity in Latin America*. New York: Friendship Press, 1980.*

Birch, Bruce. *What Does the Lord Require? The Old Testament Call to Social Witness*. Philadelphia: The Westminster Press, 1985.

Cone, James, H. *God of the Oppressed*. New York: Seabury Press, 1975.

Craig, Mary. *Six Modern Martyrs*. New York: The Crossroad Publishing Company, 1985.

Gutierrez, Gustavo. *A Theology of Liberation*. Maryknoll, New York: Orbis Press, 1973.

Moede, Gerald F. *God's Power and Our Weakness*. Princeton, New Jersey: Consultation on Church Union, 1982.

Tamez, Elsa. *Bible of the Oppressed*. Maryknoll, New York: Orbis Books, 1982.

Together on the Way, The Story of the Dialogue between the Churches of the United States and the Soviet Union. Copies of this important document are available from the US-USSR Church Relations Committee, National Council of the Churches of Christ, Room 800, 475 Riverside Drive, New York, N.Y. 10115.

Tutu, Desmond. *Hope and Suffering*. Grand Rapids, Michigan: William B. Eerdmans Publishing Company, 1984.*

---

* Available from the Service Center. Check current *Catalog* for ordering information.

CHAPTER IV

FAMINE—HUNGER

The time is coming, says the Lord God,
when I will send famine on the land,
not hunger for bread or thirst for water,
but for hearing the word of the Lord.

Amos 8:11 (NEB)

This death notice appeared in a German newspaper on November 13, 1981:

DEATH NOTICE

Of the 120 million children born in 1979, the year of the child, more than 16 million have experienced hunger.

Today, November 13, 1981, on the first day of Peace Week,

15,000 HUMAN BEINGS

are dying of hunger.

And on this day the rest of us are spending 1.4 billion dollars for military weapons.

We are grieving.

Isolde and Bartel

with Saskia (2 1/2 yrs. old) and Maren (1).[1]

A report entitled "Unfed America, 1985," by the respected organization *Bread for the World*, claims that 1.5 million people are going hungry every day *in this country* and that federal food programs lack adequate funding to meet the needs of hungry Americans. The survey was conducted in 36 cities and counties by volunteers who take part in an ongoing food monitoring project called *Hunger Watch U.S.A.*

An inescapable quality of being human is experiencing hunger. The natural body mechanism of stomach pangs or a slight headache make us uncomfortably aware of the need for food. Under normal circumstances, we take in food and

---

[1] Dorothee Soelle and Fulbert Steffensky, *Not Just Yes & Amen, Christians with a Cause* (Philadelphia: Fortress Press, 1985), p. 14. Copyright © 1983 by Rohwohlt Taschenbuch Verlag, Federal Republic of Germany. English translation copyright © 1985. Used by permission.

the body is satisfied until the cycle begins again a few hours later.

"Famished" suggests hunger to the point of actual suffering. The root of the word "famished" is taken from "famine"—one of the three dreaded scourges of human history. While famine ordinarily means starvation from an acute shortage of food, it is important for those Christians who live outside of the world hunger belt to consider the consequences of a spiritual famine as well.

"Hunger" is a word that can be used to indicate "a great longing for," that is, a yearning for something that is highly desired but missing in life. Scripture uses "hunger" in this latter sense when Jesus says, "Blessed are those who hunger and thirst for righteousness, for they shall be satisfied" (Matthew 5:6). An individual may be spiritually deprived as well as physically malnourished. There are signs that vital spiritual nutrients are missing from many lives. The mission of the church includes working to alleviate both physical and spiritual hunger.

A Bible Study on the Word "Famine"

Famine is a killer that is stalking our modern world, even as it has done from the beginning of human history. A word study from Bible may be a helpful starting point. Word studies are fun to do together. A word study can also illuminate a topic by opening up all of the scripture texts in a new and fresh way.

How to Do a Biblical Word Study:

You will need a complete concordance to the Bible. I used the *Nelson's Complete Concordance on the Revised Standard Version* for my study. I also read two study translations for comparison. The two texts I worked with were *The New English Bible with the Apocrypha, Oxford Study Edition* and *The Oxford Annotated Bible with the Apocrypha, Revised Standard Version*.[2] A Bible dictionary is helpful. I also supplemented my study with information from *Collier's Encyclopedia* and other sources that will be listed in the footnotes.

---

[2] For a complete method of doing biblical word studies consult Robin Maas, *Church Bible Study Handbook* (Nashville: Abingdon, 1982).

1. Begin by looking up the word "famine" in the concordance. Note how many times the word appears in the Old Testament and how many times in the New Testament.
2. What are the books in which the word appears the most times? Count the number of times the word appears. What does it indicate if the word appears many times and seems to be widespread throughout the scripture?
3. Begin to look up the word "famine." Be sure and read the footnotes in the study Bibles. The footnotes in both the Oxford study edition of the Revised Standard Version and the New English Bible will give you much helpful information.
4. The notes in the study Bibles will suggest other scriptures that relate to the particular passage you are exploring. Cross reference some of these passages; that is, trace those passages pointed to in the footnotes.
5. Jot down information as you go along. Finally, draw up a list of conclusions from your word study and share with your group.

Here is what I discovered as I explored the word "famine." There are over one hundred references to the word "famine" in the Old and New Testament beginning with Genesis 12:10, "There came a famine in the land, so severe that Abram went down to Egypt to live there for a while." It is amazing how many of the major events in biblical history were affected by acute food shortages. Famine forced Isaac to move his family into the land of the Philistines. He prospered there, with so many flocks and herds and slaves that the Philistines were envious of his power and asked Isaac to move back home (Genesis 26).

Remember the famous vision of Pharaoh? He dreamed that while he was standing on the banks of the Nile, he saw seven fat and sleek cows and then seven different cows that were gaunt and lean. Even though the lean and gaunt cows devoured the fat cows, they remained as skinny as ever. The Hebrew slave Joseph interpreted the dreams to mean that in the near future there would be a seven-year-famine.

Famine caused Elimelech and Naomi to move to Moab, where one of their sons married Ruth. Naomi made the decision to return to Palestine after her husband's death because she had heard that "the Lord had cared for his people and given them food" (Ruth 1:6). The need for food led Ruth to glean in Boaz's field. Ruth and Boaz married and their son became the father of Jesse. Jesse was the father of David. Thus famine played a hidden role in events leading to the birth of Israel's greatest monarch.

The Bible describes events during a terrible famine in Samaria at the time of Elijah and another seven-year famine during the career of Elisha (I Kings 18:2, II Kings 8:1). Episodes of cannibalism during severe famine are disclosed in II Kings 6:26-30 and Lamentations 4:10. The ultimate tragedy of cannibalism has been recorded during severe famines throughout history.

Famine played its role in the downfall of the Southern Kingdom of Judah. Jerusalem was under seige by Nebuchadnezzar and the armies of Babylon. When mass starvation became acute, the common people threw open the city gates. King Zedekiah fled, but the Chaldean army captured the King near Jericho. Zedekiah's sons were slain before his eyes and he himself was blinded before he was carried off to exile in Babylon. After the exile, there was a famine that caused disruptions while Nehemiah tried to rebuild the walls of Jerusalem (Nehemiah 5:1-5). War and civil strife led to famine.

In David's reign there was an acute famine that lasted for three years, so he looked around for someone to blame. David consulted with the Lord (although the reader is not told how the Lord communicated to David) and announced that the "blood-guilt rested on Saul and on his family because he put the Gibeonites to death" (II Samuel 21:1). Desperate to rid his kingdom of hunger, David asked the Gibeonites how the grievance could be redressed. The Gibeonites demanded the death of seven of Saul's sons. David dutifully rounded up seven of Saul's sons and grandsons (although he kindly spared the son of his friend, Jonathan), handed them over to the Gibeonites who piously threw them over a mountain to their deaths. The male heirs of the line of Saul were ritually sacrificed to bring the rains.

From the perspective of the twentieth century, one wonders if David heard the Lord correctly. David's notion that divine wrath caused natural disasters and that the grievances of God must be appeased by a sacrifice is a very,

69

very ancient religious belief. Later in the postexilic period, annual purification rituals involved casting lots over two goats, one goat for the Lord and the other to expiate for the sins of the community. The goat who bore the sins of the people was driven alive toward the desert, away from human habitation (Leviticus 15:7-10). The great English translator of the Bible, William Tyndale, in A.D. 1530, labeled this practice of atonement the "scapegoat."

The New Testament world was severely affected by famine during the reign of Claudius (A.D. 41-54), when mass hunger spread from Judea to Greece and then as far as Italy. The early church in Antioch sent contributions "each according to his means for the relief of their fellow Christians in Judea" (Acts 11:28).

People in all cultures living in Bible times had very limited ways to explain natural disasters. The three great human tragedies listed over and over again in the scriptures are sword, famine and pestilence. These words tend to stand together in that order (Ezekiel 6:11, Jeremiah 32:24). Is there possibly a natural cause and effect between sword, pestilence and famine quite apart from the question of sin and punishment?

We know that war brings on an emergency situation where crops are destroyed and supplies cut off—a disaster in any culture that is without refrigeration or natural stores of food. Famine is still the result of prolonged warfare. Pestilence is a catch-all term for an infectious or contagious disease that inevitably follows famine. The bubonic plague, carried by fleas from infected rats, ravaged Europe following the famine of 1347. The carnage of war, multiple deaths by starvation and unsanitary conditions bring communicable diseases in its wake.

Events during the reign of David point to the intimate connection between war, famine and pestilence. The books of I and II Samuel record continual strife. Hunger was certainly the natural result of constant disruption in agriculture. Sometime after the sacrifice of Saul's descendants, three separate wars were recorded in five verses (II Samuel 22:18-20). Following these wars was a great pestilence that killed 70,000 people. Still believing that a specific human sin must have brought the pestilence, David blamed himself for initiating an unpopular national census. It never occurred to ancient people that warfare itself was *the* sin that might be the culprit.

The pattern of war, famine and pestilence is as true in this century as it was in biblical times. A major human tragedy of World War II was the Bengal famine of 1943-1944 in India. A natural calamity, the Mindapore Cyclone, struck in the midst of the war in which rice imports were cut off from Burma. As a direct result of the famine and epidemics that followed, 1.5 million people died. More recently, blockades prevented shipments of food from reaching the region of Biafra during the Nigerian civil war of 1967-1970. More than a million Biafrans starved to death.

The explanation given by ancient peoples for drought, famine, pestilence, black or red blight, or plagues of locusts was to blame specific human sins (I Kings 8:35-53). It is questionable, however, whether any human acts (even war) always brought on the periods of drought that were common in the ancient Near East. Rainfall was marginal and irregular. Prolonged drought with crop failures is still the most common cause of famine, particularly in areas where rainfall is highly variable (although famine has been caused in temperate zones by excessive rainfall and flooding.)

Drought has always been common in semi-arid zones where rainfall is barely sufficient in normal years. The following incident occurred recently in the region of Africa just south of the Sahara desert:

> I see her standing lost in agony with a tiny baby in her arms. The area of her camp is severely affected by drought. Her child is dying quietly of thirst. In front of her—a water hole with thick, polluted water. She has a choice: to let her only baby die from dehydration or to let him drink of poisoned water. I watch her make the choice. She bends, her hand is cupped and filled with mud; she lifts it slowly to her baby's mouth.[3]

Some rains have fallen in the southern Sahara region in recent weeks, but as the shifting desert indicates, there will probably never be enough rain in that area to alleviate the

[3]Liv Ullman, *Choices* (New York: Alfred A. Knopf, 1984), p. 87. The Norwegian actress Liv Ullman has travelled for UNICEF and The International Rescue Committee.

human suffering. Is praying to God for rain a realistic response to human need in arid zones? What does it say to those praying if sufficient rains do not fall South of the Sahara? Does a lack of moisture mean that God is withholding rain, or might it indicate instead the inevitable problems of living in this very dry region? If the latter is true (climate is the culprit), then it would seem that feeding programs are an emergency relief measure and that other long-term solutions will have to be found.

This brief Bible study confirms two important facts:

First: Starvation has been a fact of life throughout all of human history. Famine has been rare only in humid tropical areas. It is not even possible to calculate the number of deaths over the years from famine and from the nutritional and communicable diseases that follow. A few statistics from the modern era make the point. Ten major famines in India between 1860 and 1900 resulted in 15 million deaths. China suffered nine million deaths between 1876 and 1879 and two million more in the famine of 1929. More than three million persons died in the Soviet Union in the famine of 1932-1933. The last great famine in Europe was in Ireland between 1846 and 1849 when short harvests caused by the potato blight led to a million deaths and to the emigration of 1.5 million persons chiefly to the United States. A million Biafrans were famine casualties in 1967-1970. We have not begun to count the millions of deaths in the Sahel region of Africa which began in the 1960's and continues into the 1980's, a famine that affects at least nine African nations![4]

Second: War, famine, disease, and oppression are interconnected afflictions that have brought misery and death throughout human history. Some periods of famine have been purely natural disasters. Unfortunately, all too often, human blunders add to the devastation. The world in witness to "the four horsemen of the apocalypse" all over again in Ethiopia.[5] Several years of drought in an already arid land

---

[4] All historical statistics on famine are found in *Collier's Encyclopedia.*

[5] The numbers are so massive and the actual process of dying from starvation is so cruel that such frightful suffering is difficult to grasp. Only strong, poetic imagery seems able to express the enormity of the tragedy. Drawing on the language of Jewish apocalypse found in Zechariah 1:7-17; 6;1-8), John of Patmos (who wrote the book of Revelation) uses different

72

has brought annual crop failures. At the same time, a civil war rages on while the government, for its own political reasons, hinders international relief efforts.

The tragic relationship between war and famine is to be seen in African feeding camps. Liv Ullmann, who travels for *UNICEF* (United Nations International Children's Educational Fund) tells of meeting a nomadic woman who had been preparing tea for her two boys as they were harvesting wood. The approaching army saw the smoke and an old woman peacefully preparing tea. As the soldiers approached, the boys ran. An army captain caught the woman by the neck and pushed her face into the fire, and holding her there stepped on her face. Guerrillas appeared and, seeing what was happening, shot toward the scene. Bullets killed not only the soldier who held her face in the fire but also killed her two sons. All of this nomadic woman's children and grandchildren had now been killed in the civil war. She escaped on a donkey and found the refugee camp with her mutilated face and burnt body. This nomadic woman and her family were surviving until they were caught as innocent victims, not of the famine but of the civil war.

In that same refugee camp, a young girl of fourteen started to give birth under a bush while her mother ran around the bush screaming in despair. When the baby boy was born after twenty-four hours of labor and the young girl nearly died, the mother just went on screaming in the desert for her daughter. The young girl, lying on the sand, was given a cover to shield her child. A doctor sewed up her torn body. The father of the baby was fighting somewhere in Ethiopia, and the new mother did not know whether he was dead or alive. The grandmother went on howling; three generations of a family on the desert sands.[6]

Were the biblical people right in their belief that human sin is the ultimate cause of hunger? One can reject the notion of a direct causal link between God's anger for specific sins which lead to a particular famine and still perceive the truth that it is human sin (strife, killing,

---

colored horses to picture the old enemies—sword, famine and pestilence. (See Revelation 6:1-17.)

[6] Liv Ullmann, *Choices*, pp. 88-94.

blockades, crop destruction, cutting off relief efforts, and indifference or hostility to the needy) that exacerbates and aggravates the droughts and disease that occur within the natural order. Experts agree that there is enough food to feed everyone in the world. The problem is not shortages of food but inadequate distribution. Mass hunger is due not only to acts of nature but also to the lack of will in people.[7]

The Predicament of the Prosperous[8]

The evidence clearly suggests that peace and justice issues belong together. It is doubtful that famine will be eliminated unless and until wars cease. Technically, that human community has the means to banish famine from the earth.[9] New technologies, surpluses from other regions and the means of transportation to bring in food quickly are all possible. Yet, we have only to look at the pictures of emaciated skeletal forms of starving bodies to know the political will has been lacking for permanent solutions to hunger.

Non-industrialized countries with inadequate reserves of foreign exchange find it difficult to finance a sharply increased volume of food. Estimates are that 500 million people world wide are constantly malnourished. Even without the dreadful famine, protein-energy malnutrition (PEM) kills 10 million people every year.[10] Millions of people in India and Bangladesh exist on a famine level.

There are hungry children in every country, including the United States. The House of Representatives Select Committee on Hunger heard a report on 23 May 1985 that kwashiorkor and marasmus—severe protein-and calorie-deficiency diseases usually seen only in Third World

---

[7] Sally Urvina, "Malnutrition in Third World Countries," *The Christian Century*, May 23, 1984, p. 550f.

[8] *The Predicament of the Prosperous* is the title of an important resource for Christians who live in a prosperous and powerful nation. Birch and Rasmussen call for a radical change in life-style for Christians in the United States and believe that "joyful austerity" and a "life of frugality" would signal a more redemptive life. Bruce C. Birch and Larry L. Rasmussen, *The Predicament of the Prosperous* (Philadelphia: The Westminster Press, 1978), p. 192.

[9] Sally Urvina, "Malnutrition," p. 550f.

[10] Sally Urvina, "Malnutrition", p. 550.

countries—have been reported in Illinois, Texas and New Mexico. Sixteen cases of kwashiorkor and marasmus have been documented recently at Children's Memorial Hospital in Chicago, along with other cases of less extreme nutritional deprivation among poor children.[11] It simply is not truthful to think that severe hunger exists only in poorer countries.

Pessimists often quote Jesus, who said, "You will have the poor among you always" (Matthew 26:11). The context for this statement is a rebuke of the disciples for questioning the wisdom of the unnamed woman who anoints Jesus. The disciples question her use of expensive oil by piously contending that the money could have been given to the poor. Jesus understood the woman's sign-actions as a prophetic recognition of himself as the Messiah, the Anointed One. The disciples may have had good motives, but they missed the profound religious significance of her action. The issue at that moment was not the use of money or the fate of the poor.

Jesus likely was remembering an important passage from the Torah, "The poor will always be with you in the land. . . ", but in this context, he did not finish the whole sentence which reads, "the poor will always be with you in the land, and for that reason I command you to be open-handed with your countrymen, both poor and distressed, in your own land" (Deuteronomy 15:11). An earlier passage in the same chapter is even more optimistic, "There will never be any poor among you if only you obey the Lord your God by carefully keeping these commandments which I lay upon you this day" (Deuteronomy 15:4-5).

Understanding and keeping God's commandments with regard to the poor is one of the predicaments of prosperous Christians in our day. There is an ongoing argument in many churches between those who believe: (a) that individual gifts to the poor and the generous charity of a denomination can make an enormous difference in individual lives; (b) and those who assert that there is only value in focusing our energies on changing the political and economic systems that allow hunger and starvation.

---

[11] Spencer Rich, "Third World Diseases Noted in U.S.," *The Washington Post*, 24 May, 1985.

Whatever the ultimate strategy, the suffering neighbors know the compassion of God through our solidarity with their need. Church World Service regularly calls for congregations to make blankets. In my Annual Conference, colorful baby blankets often line the walls of the auditorium, the gifts of United Methodist Women. I always hope that some of those blankets will go to the refugee camps in Somalia. I once held the illusion that Africa is always warm. From one refugee camp in Somalia, however, comes this verbal picture:

> If you walk the camp at around six in the morning, the air is chilly and you will see small, thin bodies shivering. Children are about to die because even blankets are a luxury here. Little children sleeping close—oh so close to each other. As if they only can find warmth in other bodies as weak and thin as their own. I wonder what they dream.[12]

Warm blankets made for the babies in refugee camps is an example of service-oriented mission. The blankets are absolutely essential and will help individual children survive the cold nights. But it would be a mistake to believe that such gifts absolve the church from its responsibility to change the conditions that bring children into such camps in the first place.

Sometimes we prosperous Christians argue so much among ourselves about the best way to help alleviate hunger that we alienate others from the good will so necessary to bring about change. Religious writer Monica Furlong argues that "guilt will not move us to feed the poor,"[13] and it is doubtful that accusing each other of bad faith will either. Jesus taught believers that all those in need (regardless) are our neighbors and are to be helped (Luke 19:29-37). Urgent conversations are needed between Christians of all political persuasions to devise effective and cooperative strategies for meeting the crisis of physical hunger.

Anorexia: A First World Tragedy

A startled world learned of the sudden death of popular singer Karen Carpenter. Karen and her brother Richard,

---

[12] Liv Ullman, *Choices*, p. 90.
[13] Monica Furlong, *Traveling In* (Crowley Publications, 1984), pp. 79-84.

who recorded under the byline, "The Carpenters," seemed to be healthy, attractive young adults. Days passed before press reports hinted that Karen may have died of complications linked to an eating disorder called *anorexia nervosa*.

A mysterious and frightening illness that leaves its victims looking as if they had emerged from a concentration camp, anorexia nervosa is a form of self-starvation. The problem is said to be a growing epidemic among young women in their late teens. Only about ten percent of the cases are young males, but they are less likely to recover from the disease. Estimates claim that anorexia afflicts one out of every 200 adolescent girls between the ages twelve and twenty-two.[14] The profile of anorexic youth is particularly frightening for the middle-class. Although anorexic young people come from all socio-economic classes and all races, the majority tend to be affluent, white, female, and high achievers in school.

Without proper treatment, up to 20 percent of those with anorexia will die from the irreversible effects of starvation; others may develop lifelong health problems. In addition, six times as common as anorexia are the related eating disorders of bulimia and bulimarexia in which the victim either alternates cycles of starving and overeating or consumes enough calories each day but vomits nearly all of them up to avoid a weight gain.

The disease seems to be related to the message of thinness as a standard of beauty for women in a culture with an abundance of food. Thinness is pursued by relentless dieting until the anorexic youth no longer counts calories out of choice but out of compulsion. Anorexia appears to be a type of revenge on the body in the losing competition for thinness. Eventually the desperate body begins feeding off its own muscle tissue, including vital organs, until, if untreated, the patient becomes too weak to survive. Like the victims of protein-energy malnutrition (PEM) in

---

[14] Information for the section is taken from Steven Levenkron, *Treating and Overcoming Anorexia Nervosa* (New York: Charles Scribner's Sons, 1982) and Janice M. Cauwels, *Bulimia, The Binge-Purge Compulsion* (Garden City, New York: Doubleday and Company, Inc., 1983).

developing countries, one of the adverse effects of malnutrition is that the body becomes unable to defend itself against infection. The anorexic behaves increasingly as a starving person does anywhere in the world, but unlike her counterpart in Ethiopia, she denies the starvation and refuses food.

An enormous amount of money is spent by this society on diet products, cosmetics and related beauty aids (including cosmetic surgery to change the body) each year. The self-inflicted starvation of young women in our culture of plenty seems to be a demonic reversal of the images of undernourished young mothers holding wizened, skeletal children in a culture of famine. Anorexia is a pathological exaggeration of the preoccupation with a beautiful body in an atmosphere of plenty, just as PEM (protein-energy malnutrition) is an exaggeration of the extremes of a culture limited in resources.[15]

Anorexia is only one of the symptoms of spiritual starvation among youth in the United States. More than one million runaway children, with a median age of 15, are estimated to be on the streets in this country, according to a report published in the 18 August 1985 issue of *Parade*. About 70 percent of these runaways are white and an overwhelming number are from middle and upper class families.

A subcommittee of the Education Commission of the States reported in the 2 November 1985 issue of *The Washington Post* that at least 15 percent of adolescent Americans between the ages of 16 and 19 are "disconnected" from society as a result of drug abuse, delinquency, pregnancy, unemployment and dropping out of school. The study concluded that by conservative estimates 1,250,000 white youths, 750,000 black youths and 375,000 Hispanic 16 to 19 year olds are moving into this disconnected state. What is the mission of the church for the kind of human hunger that puts so many of our nation's young people at risk?

---

[15] The connection between starvation in a culture of plenty and in a culture with limited resources, was first suggested to me by a sermon preached in the chapel at Wesley Theological Seminary by a senior student who had married a woman with anorexia nervosa.

The Suffering Compassion of God

God cares for and suffers with both the undernourished young mothers in refugee camps and the malnourished young adults who voluntarily vomit their food. God is the kind of God who sings a lament for the suffering ones, for those who physically and mentally hunger and thirst. In the words of the prophet Jeremiah (9:21-22):

> For the wound of the daughter of my people is my heart
> wounded.
> I mourn, and dismay has taken hold of me.
> Is there no balm in Gilead?
> Is there no physician there?
> Why then has the health of the daughter of my people
> not been restored?
> O that my head were water,
> and my eyes a fountain of tears,
> that I might weep day and night
> for the slain of the daughter of my people!

Yahweh weeps bitterly over Israel as surely as Rachel, the ancient mother, laments the exile of the northern nation (Jeremiah 31:15-20).[16] What kind of a God is this who suffers with the victims of hunger, poverty or oppression? Over and over the Old Testament confesses a God who is righteous and brings justice to the wronged; a God who is compassionate and gracious, long suffering and ever constant; a God slow to anger, who will not nurse anger for all time but who by no means clears the guilty; a God whose faithful, steadfast love endures for ever (Exodus 34:6-7; Psalm 103:6-18; Psalm 145:8).[17] The Psalmist declares that God's eyes are turned toward those who hope for the unfailing love of God "to deliver them from death, to keep them alive in famine" (Psalm 33:18-19).

The emotion of compassion attributed to God in Psalm

---

[16] Claus Westermann, *Elements of Old Testament Theology*, translated by Douglas W. Sottt (Atlanta: John Knox Press, 1982) p. 132. Also see Phyllis Trible, *God and the Rhetoric of Sexuality* (Philadelphia: Fortress Press, 1978), pp. 34-56.

[17] On the compassion of God see the work of Terence E. Fretheim, *The Suffering of God, An Old Testament Perspective* in *Overtures to Biblical Theology* (Philadelphia: Fortress Press, 1984).

103 is an attribute to be found throughout the Old Testament. The story goes that after the man and woman were driven from the Garden of Eden, God made tunics of skins and clothed them—a sign of mercy. Abraham Heschel believes that the compassionate suffering of God, "the God of pathos," is a central category of the prophetic understanding.[18] The Bible consistently affirms that God suffers with suffering people.

God was present *with* Jesus suffering on the cross. God was present *for us* through Jesus suffering on the cross. Jesus stands with all who suffer from hunger as one who knows the final agony of human death, a death caused by the inhumanity, injustice and indifference of his neighbors.

We Are Called to Be Bread Bakers

There is no social blueprint to be found in the Bible. The scriptures are clear, however, that God has a special concern for the poor, the hungry and the alienated. Once that priority is established, "then you have to work out for yourself, as honestly and intelligently as you can, how, within the structure of the society you live in, you can best implement that concern."[19] Theologian Robert McAfee Brown gives us a helpful "handle" to understand the Christian mission in what he calls the *"Therefore Variation."*[20]

The early Christians believed that they were impelled to love one another because "God first loved us." God loves us, *therefore* we must love one another (I John 4:19). Again and again in the scriptures we read that because Yahweh is a just God, the people also should be righteous. The word "therefore" is the pivot of the ethical position. God is compassionate, *therefore* the right motive for feeding bodies and souls is to follow in the context of what God has done in Jesus Christ.

The physically hungry need bread—or gruel—or any of the other high protein grain products that will keep them

---

[18] Heschel, *Prophets*, p. 223.
[19] Robert McAfee Brown, *The Bible Speaks to You* (Philadelphia: The Westminster Press, 1965), p. 284.
[20] Brown, *The Bible Speaks to You*, pp. 237-240.

alive. The spiritually hungry, those whose lives are empty and undernourished, need the bread of life. The writer of the Gospel of John calls Jesus "the bread of life." According to John, Jesus declares himself to be the living bread when he says, "I give it for the life of the world" (John 6:22-58). Therefore, Christians must follow their Lord and become bread bakers for the world.

The sharing of bread has stood at the center of the Christian community from the beginning of the church (Acts 2:42-47). When the community breaks bread together at the Eucharist (Holy Communion) and remembers the farewell meal (Jesus took bread, blessed it, broke it, and gave it to his friends saying "this is my body."), at that moment, Jesus' story becomes our story and his compassion our compassion. As the Church eats together the broken bread and drinks from the cup, the risen Christ is "present-with-us," healing our brokenness and binding our wounds.

Jesus gives us living bread and therefore we are challenged to become bread bakers for a needy world.[21] What a wonderful image—to become God's bread bakers, providing physical or spiritual nourishment wherever and whenever there is need.

The biographer of Thomas Merton, writer Monica Furlong, warns us, however, that we must be careful not to spiritualize suffering or overly romanticize our role in bringing relief.[22] If we are made to feel guilty about those things over which we have little control, (the famine in Africa or slave trading in the 18th century, for example), "it makes it easier to avoid facing the things which *are* our fault." Christians will be more effective, Furlong contends, if we learn to deal with real guilt and not "cheap" or false guilt. Sometimes it is possible to conceal our own inner suffering from ourselves by projecting

---

[21] Bread and potatoes go together. One energetic hunger program, called *The Society of St. Andrew*, is less than two years old but has managed to salvage and distribute over eighteen and a half million pounds of potatoes to feed the hungry. A project of the Virginia Annual Conference, it began because Christians observed the massive waste of discarded potatoes and had both the creative imagination and the commitment to make the project work.

[22] Furlong, *Traveling In*, chapter IX.

it onto more general human problems. By learning how to enter into the heart of our own suffering and bearing the pain of people around us in our community, we will learn to be effective healers. It is important to learn, as Furlong suggests, to "inhabit the square foot on which one stands." We will probably be the most effective "bread bakers," and "system shakers" in our own community.

Local congregations also need to support the mission of national boards and agencies as they work on global issues of peace and justice. The general boards often call us to rally to specific human need elsewhere in the world. Then we generously follow the example of the early Christian community in Antioch. During a severe famine during the reign of Claudius, the church decided that members would send as much money as they could afford to help their fellow believers who lived in Judea. They sent the money to the church elders by Barnabas and Saul (Acts 11:27-30).

The poem by Alla Campbell-Bozarth expresses the thought that perhaps we ourselves are the loaf of bread, baked by a Bakerwoman God for the common communion of all peoples.

Bakerwoman God

Bakerwoman God,
I am your living bread.
Strong, brown, Bakerwoman God,
I am your low, soft and being-
    shaped loaf.
I am your rising bread, well-kneaded
    by some divine and knotty pair of
    knuckles, by your warm earth-hands.
I am bread well-kneaded.

Put me in your fire, Bakerwoman God,
put me in your own bright fire.

I am warm, warm as you from fire.
I am white and gold, soft and hard,
    brown and round.
I am so warm from fire.

Break me, Bakerwoman God.
I am broken under your caring Word.
Drop me in your special juice in pieces.

Drop me in your blood.
Drunken me in the great red flood.
Self-giving chalice, swallow me.
My skin shines in the divine wine.
My face is cup-covered and I drown.

I fall up in a red pool
　　in a gold world
　　where your warm sunskin hand is there
　　to catch and hold me
Bakerwoman God, remake me.[23]

Questions for Discussion

1. How do you think God is related to the suffering caused by weather, pests and diseases that seem to be a part of the world order?

2. Should we pray for rain to solve the problem of famine in arid desert regions? If sufficient moisture is not possible from the environment, what creative solutions would you devise for dealing with what appears to be inevitable starvation?

3. Do you agree with the author that famine, disease and war are interconnected? Discuss the examples given in the chapter. What can the church do to prevent this ancient scourge?

4. What are the two approaches to the mission of the church discussed in this chapter? Do you see one method as more effective than the other? Does your congregation engage in a service and charity-oriented approach to mission? Does your congregation work to change the conditions and environment that make physical and spiritual hunger such a problem in this country and in the world? Would it be helpful for your church to engage in both approaches to mission at the same time? What would be the advantage in engaging in acts of charity *and* working toward changing unjust systems?

5. Do you agree with Monica Furlong that "guilt will not move us to feed the poor"? Why or why not? Can you give examples of your answers from your own lives?

---

[23] Campbell-Bozarth, Alla. "Bakerwoman God," in *In God's Image: Toward Wholeness for Women and Men*. New York: Lutheran Church in America, 1976. Used by permission.

Spiritual Exercise

Bread Connections[24]

The breaking of bread can become an expression of solidarity with all who suffer, whether nearby or far away—a sign opening us up to the whole of humanity. Christians should regularly break bread together and use those occasions to make "bread connections." Making a "bread connection" means intentionally letting the sign-action of breaking bread become a way of bringing the bread bakers and bread eaters into prayer contact with people whose bodies have been broken by oppression or starvation. Bread connections raise our consciousness and challenge us to work for the daily bread of all people.

Making a Bread Connection

1. Bake some beautiful loaves of homemade bread. At the same time, make a pot of gruel from a grain product (such as farina). Do not use any additives such as salt or sugar.

2. At the conclusion of your study session, spread a cloth on a table, light an oil lamp (or a candle), and place the gruel and bread on the table. The gruel will be cold. Have bowls for each participant on the table but no utensils or napkins.

3. As the members gather around the table, ladle out a portion of gruel and give a bowl to each member. Instruct the group to eat some of the gruel with their fingers as a leader reads aloud to the group some of experiences of Liv Ullmann from the above chapter.

After each of the short readings, stop and give a name to the unnamed sufferers in the readings. Give a name (any name the group chooses) to the mother who was forced to give her son polluted water, a name to the older woman whose face was burned in the fire, a name to the fourteen-year-old in the labors of childbirth and one to her screaming mother.

---

[24] The concept of "bread connections" is the idea of Donald P. McNeill, Douglas A. Morrison and Henri J. M. Nouwen in *Compassion, A Reflection on the Christian Life* (Garden City, New York: Doubleday & Company, 1982), p. 115.

4. Name these unnamed refugees before God and say a prayer for all the millions of hungry refugees in the world.

5. Read John 6:30-35. Break the bread and give each person a good hunk in their bowls. After the group is instructed to eat the broken bread, a leader should tell all present to enjoy and savor the experience of eating. Choosing freely to follow a compassionate God is the right reason for making "bread connections." In addition to embracing compassion as a life-style, Christians are also free to celebrate the bounty of a good God.

6. Pass around a towel so that people may wipe their hands. The group should be reminded that napkins and towels are a great luxury in many parts of the world.

7. At this point, the leader might remind the group of the passage from Galatians 5:9, which reads, "a little leaven, remember, leavens all the dough." Small, individual acts of charity are not lost in what seems to be the endless hunger in the world. A money contribution for famine relief, a blanket made for an unknown child, becoming a "crisis foster parent" for a troubled youth in your town are "a little leaven that leavens all the dough."

8. Conclude by praying the ecumenical version of the Lord's Prayer. Be especially aware of the two petitions, for one's "daily bread" and to be saved from the "time of trial and delivered from evil."

> Our Father in heaven,
> Holy is your name.
> Your Kingdom come, your will be done
>   on earth as it is in heaven.
> Give us today our daily bread.
> And forgive us our sins
>   as we forgive those who sin against us.
> Save us from the time of trial
> And deliver us from evil.
> For the Kingdom, the power and the glory are yours,
> Now and Forever. Amen.[25]

---

[25] This text of Lord's Prayer is the widely used ecumenical translation prepared by the International Commission on English Texts.

Further Reading

Birch, Bruce C. and Rasmussen, Larry L. *The Predicament of the Prosperous*. Philadelphia: The Westminster Press, 1978.

Furlong, Monica. *Travelling In*. U.S.A.: Crowley Publications, 1984.

Gerstenberger, Erhard S. and Schrage, Wolfgang. *Suffering*. Nashville: Abingdon, 1980.

Hunger in a Land of Plenty, A Study and Action Guide. Study and Leader's Guide from *Bread for the World*, 802 Rhode Island Avenue, N.E. Washington D.C. 20018. *Bread for the World* has available two other important studies: *A Hungry World* and *Land and Hunger: A Biblical Worldview*.

McNeill, Donald P., Morrison, Dougas A., and Nouwen, Henri J. M. *Compassion, A Reflection On The Christian Life*. Garden City: New York: Doubleday & Company, 1982.

Soelle, Dorothee and Steffensky, Fulbert. *Not Just Yes & Amen, Christians With a Cause*. Philadelphia: Fortress Press, 1985.

Stromberg, Jean, ed. *Sharing One Bread, Sharing One Mission, The Eucharist as Missionary Event*. Geneva: World Council of Churches, 1983.

Ullmann, Liv. *Choices*. New York: Alfred A. Knopf, 1984.

Chapter V

TANGLES—POWERLESSNESS

So she lulled him to sleep, wove the seven loose locks of his hair into the warp, and drove them tight with the beater, and cried, "The Philistines are upon you, Samson!" (Judges 16:14, NEB)

In the beginning it "sneaks up like a thief."[1] The disease moves progressively from an inability to remember, to write checks properly, or to do simple math to a total shut-down of the mind. The victim becomes essentially "brainless" but otherwise may be physically healthy. The illness was named after Alois Alzheimer, a German neurologist, who in 1906 discovered clumps of twisted nerve-cell fibers in the brain of a 51-year-old woman who showed all the signs of senility associated with old age. He called these twisted fibers "neurofibrillary tangles."[2]

Concentrated in the cerebral cortex and hippocampus, centers of memory and intellectual activity, minute threads of protein from nerve cells are twisted into a "double helix" or paired tangles. The basic ingredient of all life, DNA, also is understood to be like two ribbons in spiral motion, that is, a double helix.

The double helix is the symbol for all organic life. In a brain afflicted by Alzheimer's, it seems as if nature is playing a cruel joke and that the basic language of life has gone crazy. An image that comes to mind is that of an old-fashioned telephone switchboard in which all the cords have become tangled and plugged into the wrong holes so that all the messages are garbled.

In addition to the tangles, plaques form outside the nerve cells. A neuropathologist describes the plaques "like

---

[1] Charles Leroux, "The Silent Epidemic," part I (*The Chicago Tribune*, 1981 reprinted by The Alzheimer's Disease and Related Disorders Association Inc. ADRDA National Headquarters, 360 N. Michigan Avenue, Suite 601, Chicago, Illinois 60601.

[2] See the feature article in the 3 December 1984 *Newsweek*, "A Slow Death of the Mind," pp. 56-62.

mothholes in fabric, like the footprints of an elephant across a wheatfield, destructive."[3] He continues:

If you were inside an Alzheimer's brain, it would look like someone had been loose with a shotgun in there, but it's really more akin to someone taking a hatchet to telephone cables. The flow of information inside the brain is disrupted.

The hideousness of what happens to the Alzheimer's brain is worse than any Stephen King horror story. Spouses and children are totally powerless against its quiet, relentless onslaught. Even more horrifying is the knowledge that children of the victims may have a four times greater chance of developing the disease than the rest of the general population.[4] It will stealthily creep upon the children as secretly as it did upon their parents. My mother-in-law, who was once a bright, energetic teacher, has the disease as did her mother before her. My husband looked on helplessly at the mental deterioration of his maternal grandmother and now his mother. He worries about his own future.

A diagnosis of "cancer" strikes terror in the hearer because that word sounds like a death sentence. The word "cancer" shakes away our complacency and renders us vulnerable. A runaway cancerous cell in our system "invades the well-ordered society of cells surrounding it, colonizes distant areas and, as a finale in its cannibalistic orgy of flesh consuming flesh, commits suicide by destroying its host."[5] The fear of this possible death people spend much energy in the denial of death, we are as powerless against this ancient enemy of life as were all the generations before us.[6]

---

[3] Charles Leroux, part II, "In Research as in the Brain, Alzheimer's Takes a Twisting Trail."

[4] Robert N. Butler and Marian Emr, "Alzheimer's Disease: An Examination" (Chicago, Illinois: Alzheimer's Disease and Related Disorders Association, Inc.), p. 4.

[5] Pat McGrady, "The Savage Cell" quoted in Robert F. Weaver, "The Cancer Puzzle," National Geographic, September, 1976, p. 396.

[6] See Ernest Becker's Pulitzer Prize winning book The Denial of Death (New York: The Free Press, a Division of Macmillan Publishing Company Inc., 1973).

It is fascinating that medical experts now believe that the folklore of the werewolves and vampires of Transylvania, once dreaded personifications of evil, may have been based on the real victims of a rare hereditary blood disease called "porphyria." Porphyria is caused by a malfunction in the production of heme, the red pigment in blood. This blood disease, porphyria, creates extreme sensitivity to sunlight so that its victims must stay indoors and only come out at night. Exposure to light causes the skin to be disfigured by sores, and the lesions may be so severe that the nose and fingers are destroyed. The disease also causes excessive hairiness. As the skin of the lips and gums stretch and tighten, the teeth become more prominent and look like fangs.[7] Today, the rare but incurable disorder affects one in every 200,000 individuals. The disease runs in families. Perhaps an infected family once seemed to haunt a large, spooky castle during an age more superstitious than our own. Can you imagine how frightened such a family must have been in the days before enlightened medical knowledge?

Not only must we work to solve the riddle of older diseases, but also of new devastating illnesses that continue to develop in human bodies. For example, just as the World Health Organization announced that smallpox was eradicated in 1980, along came AIDS (Acquired Immune Deficiency Syndrome), which usually kills its victims within two years of diagnosis. No one has ever recovered from AIDS.

AIDS (as well as smallpox, polio, mumps, measles and the common cold) is caused by a virus. Some of the strangest objects in the natural world, viruses "lie between life and non-life."[8] There are thousands of different kinds of viruses with as many different shapes and sizes. The bacteriophage virus looks like a lunar ladder in our space program, whereas a mumps virus resembles a plate of

---

[7] Jean Seligmann with Susan Katz, "Vampire Diagnosis: Real Sick," *Newsweek*, 10 June 1985, p. 72.

[8] Information on viruses is taken from an article by Boyce Rensberger, "Viruses: The Lifeless Invaders that Enslave Cells and Kill Us," *The Washington Post*, 18 August 1985. Also see the diagram of an AIDS virus attacking the human immune system in *Time*, 12 August 1985, p. 43.

spaghetti. No matter their form, viruses invade living cells and release genetic instructions (either DNA or RNA) to force the cell to manufacture more viruses like themselves. The chemical messages are read and obeyed by the healthy cell. Unless there is an intervention to kill the invader, the result is mechanically predictable and a person with AIDS (or smallpox) will die. Persons develop AIDS, not because they are homosexual or heterosexual, but because they have been infected by a killer virus. The point is that viruses are a part of the natural order of creation. Even with advanced medical technology, human beings are still powerless against the onslaught of destructive diseases.

Powerlessness and Evil[9]

Braided brains, cannibalistic cancer cells, lunar-landing viruses and fang-like mouths have come to represent, for me, contemporary symbols of evil more surely than any of the grotesque gargoyles carved on Gothic Cathedrals. These symbols represent diseases that kill the body and the spirit in ways that, as far as we know, are not necessary for biological survival. M. Scott Peck has a useful definition of evil in his popular book *People of the Lie:*

> For the moment I can do no better than to heed my son, who, with the characteristic vision of eight-year olds, explained simply, "Why Daddy, evil is 'live' spelled backwards." Evil is in opposition to life. It is that which opposes the life force.

> Specifically, it has to do with murder—namely, unnecessary killing, killing that is not required for biological survival. . . . Evil is also that which kills the spirit . . . . that force, residing either inside or outside of human beings, that seeks to kill life. . . .[10]

Theologians John Cobb and David Griffin contend that evil "is experienced as an overwhelming destructive power

---

[9] An excellent interpretation of several Christian explanations for evil, with an eye on Jungian psychology, is found in John A. Sanford, *Evil, The Shadow Side of Reality* (New York: The Crossroad Publishing Company, 1981).

[10] M. Scott Peck, *People of the Lie: The Hope for Healing Human Evil* (New York: Simon and Schuster, 1983), pp. 42-43.

against which we find ourselves quite helpless."[11] The Christian Church has entertained several explanations for the existence of evil throughout its history. There is no single teaching that has received the endorsement of the whole community of faith. Three important answers are represented by the traditions of *dualism, privation,* and *process.*[12]

Dualism

Cyclones and tornados are capricious. That is, they change abruptly and strike at random. Innocent persons in Bangladesh, Ohio and Pennsylvania were powerless recently against savage winds. A survivor was quoted in the 10 June 1985 issue of *Newsweek:* "This was not God's work—it was the work of Satan." One does not have to personify this violently whirling column of air as the work of an actual spiritual being alien to God (Satan) to understand her distress at the utter meaninglessness of the destruction. Understanding the scientific reasons for such winds is not much comfort when your house has been destroyed.

Many Christians have believed in a dualistic view of the universe in which there is an evil power battling against the power of the goodness of God.[13] Dualism takes evil very seriously. While ultimate dualism provides an understandable explanation for evil (an adversary battling against God) and seems to take God off the hook (God is not responsible for evil and ultimately will be victorious), it has never been an attractive option for me. A Satanic figure raises more questions for me than it answers. If God is ultimately powerful, then why were demons created in the first place? Why does God continue to permit their existence? Who was it that originally tempted Satan?

---

[11] John B. Cobb, Jr. and David Ray Griffin, *Process Theology, an Introductory Exposition* (Philadelphia: The Westminster Press, 1976), p. 118.

[12] Clearly these systems of thought are much more complicated than can be developed here. This brief summary will focus on evil as seen through the doctrine of creation. No attempt is made to draw out Christological implications.

[13] For a contemporary statement of the dualistic position see Arthur C. McGill, *Suffering, A Test of Theological Method* (Philadelphia: Westminster Press, 1982).

It seems to me that human beings are quite capable of causing most of the world's problems without having to refer to a tempter. In addition, what are we to make of scripture passages that assert there are no other gods before God? Deuteronomy 32:39 is a case in point. The passage reads, "there is no god beside me: I put to death and I keep alive, I wound and I heal; there is no rescue from my grasp." In this biblical view, God is seen as controlling power and ultimately the one who is in charge of history. Whatever the cause of evil, it is consistently affirmed throughout the scriptures that God will be victorious.

I believe the survivor was mistaken in thinking that the tornado was not God's work. Sudden cracks in the earth, violent winds, lightning or meteor storms are God's work. God seems to permit creation to work its own way and apparently does not intervene in weather patterns any more than in the genetic distortions that lead to birth defects. An interesting essay by Jerald H. Jackson in the May, 1985 *Circuit Rider* makes this same point, using the "cruelties" of natural predators (lions, hyenas) to conclude, with Stephen Jay Gould, that our world is a "quirky mass of imperfections."[14]

Privation

Dualism has not been the only Christian explanation for evil.[15] There is a strong tradition in the church which claims that evil is the privation or absence of the good. This view is represented, among others, by Origen, Basil of Caesarea, Augustine and Thomas Aquinas. Good alone has substance; evil is seen to be a loss of goodness which has no life in its own right. What is experienced by humanity as wicked may be in the long run a means to the good. The bad situation may only *appear* to be evil. Thus, the loss of a friendship might only appear to be evil whereas a new and better relationship may appear in the future. Two of the greatest theologians in the early church, Origen and

---

[14] Jerald H. Jackson, "Wildness and Pastoral Care," *Circuit Rider*, May, 1985, p. 9.

[15] For a helpful discussion see "In the Shadow of Evil," in J. Philip Wogaman, *Faith and Fragmentation, Christianity for a New Age* (Philadelphia: Fortress Press, 1985), chapter 8.

Augustine, believed that evil would cease to exist at the end of time when God's plan for creation was fulfilled.

The belief that evil is the absence of good and cannot exist on its own but only by living off the good, is an interesting one in light of what we know about the operation of killer viruses. You recall that such viruses have life only as they are able genetically to reprogram healthy cells. They cease to exist when not in contact with wholeness. Still, the question of their origin and of their ultimate purpose remains.

If you are having trouble understanding the concept that evil is somehow not really "real" because it lacks substance, you will not be alone. The concept that good has "substance" belongs to another time and is a difficult one to understand in today's world. Besides, whether evil has substance or not does not diminish its terrible effects one whit. The future relationship may be worse than the one before. The doctrine that evil is the deprivation of the good has been justly criticized in that it diminishes the reality of evil. If evil can be explained away as having no substance, then the serious reality of human suffering may be overlooked and our ability weakened to recognize and deal with evil.

Process

Nature is not the only "quirky mass of imperfection." Human beings, also a part of the natural order, appear to be a "quirky *mess*." For example, there is one violent crime every twenty-four seconds in the United States. One forcible rape occurs every six minutes and one murder every twenty-three minutes.[16] One in three female children and one in seven male children will be sexually abused by the age of eighteen years.[17] American citizens are becoming accustomed to seeing the faces of millions of missing

---

[16] Statistics are from 1980 quoted by Nancy Loving "Spouse Abuse: The Hidden Crime," in *Violence Can We Outgrow It?* Published in *engage/social action*, March 1982, p. 25. *e/sa* is available from 100 Maryland Avenue, N.E. Washington, D.C. 20002.

[17] Peggy Halsey, "Abuse in the Family: Breaking the Church's Silence," A Mission/Action Study Program from the Office of Ministries With Women in Crisis, 1984, p. 2.

children on the sides of milk cartons and on television specials. Violence is at intolerable levels in our civilized society. If adults feel frightened and powerless, imagine how abused or missing children must feel.

When Idi Amin fell from power in Uganda in April, 1979, his luxurious presidential mansion revealed a chamber of horrors. In the bottom floor of the mansion that Idi Amin "stocked with board games, electronic gadgets, sports equipment and wind-up toys lay a chamber reserved for his more brutal passions: torture, mutilation and murder."[18] When authorities reached this basement lair, they found hundreds of corpses executed in a drainage gutter (in order that the floors would not be bloodied). Amin's henchmen, clad in colored sport shirts and wearing sunglasses, hacked, slashed, mutilated and tortured thousands in that dungeon during his eight-year reign. Idi Amin is still alive and well, hiding in the Middle East.

The Idi Amins and Adolf Hitlers represent an archetypal human evil that both shocks and fascinates us. Was there some monstrous genetic error in the creation of such persons? Or is it true, as the great contemporary psychologist, C. G. Jung, once wrote, that we become what we do? John A. Sanford believes that "the deliberate decision to *do* evil leads to our becoming evil." This is why, he declares, that if we live out our darkest impulses we can easily become absorbed in the "shadow side of reality."[19] Is the human race powerless against such monstrous people?

The twentieth-century school of thought known as process theology has an interesting variation on the more ancient explanations for evil.[20] In process thought, God is a dynamic "entity" who, by definition, is creative-responsive love. The creative power of divine love continually affects the created order and pulls it toward depths of complexity, harmony and justice.

The entire cosmos is still in the process of becoming.

---

[18] *Newsweek*, 23 April 1979, pp. 41-42.

[19] John A. Sanford, *Evil, The Shadow Side of Reality*, p. 105.

[20] John B. Cobb, Jr. and David Ray Griffin, *Process Theology, an Introductory Exposition* (Philadelphia: The Westminster Press, 1976) and Marjorie Hewitt Suchocki, *God, Christ, Church, A Practical Guide to Process Theology* (New York: Crossroad Publishing Company, 1982).

Natural disasters are a part of this developing universe. The end is not yet determined and process theologians declare that the "future is open." Even God does not fully know the future and therefore, does not wholly control the world. It must be noted, however, that the locus for justice is in the very nature of God. God's will may be thwarted for a time, but both the vision and the reality of *shalom* will prevail in God who is its source. Process theologians declare that God acts with the world as it is, while luring it toward its true destiny, which is, the full potential of what it can become. Evil is real but not necessary in this changing and developing world order.

God also moves human beings to become the best that their potential allows. The creative influence of God aims at promoting the good of all creatures. Even though God's power is the most effective force that exists, it does not operate by controlling the outcome. Divine love works by persuasion and not by domination. Because love is not coercive, finite creatures have the freedom to refuse to respond—to say "No!" to God's purposes. Individuals have the capacity either to opt for relatedness or for a state of alienation from God, self and one another.

What determines how a person will choose? Some interpreters of process theology closely identify evil with socialization, the process through which a person learns life patterns and meanings. The past is seen to be the conveyer of sin and demonic forces. Evil (the demonic) precedes the individual and is carried from one generation to another through the social structures of home, school, and the culture at large. Each individual has the possibility of following the old sins of past generations or to proceed toward the new, more positive future that God is creating.[21]

The process position is compelling in several ways. First,

---

[21] On the one hand, the process model is highly rationalistic. That is to say, there are reasonable explanations suggested for various types of apparent evil. On the other, process theologians operate with a highly speculative notion of the nature of God that is theoretical and not at all verifiable. I have doubts about any system of speculative thought that moves very far from faith statements into claiming exact knowledge. This is as true for process models as for the metaphysical constructs of the fourth century.

it contains the truth that the power of sin is transmitted through time and in the very structures of society. Second, process thought takes seriously the fact that evil maintains an active existence within these ever changing structures, and third, it accounts for data that suggests the world is not finished but moving toward completion. Sin and evil are seen to be a distortion of the nature of existence, a violation of the interdependence of the divine harmony.

Process does not satisfy my need, however, to understand why anomalies (that which seems to depart from the normal arrangement) exist apart from human culture. Why do killer viruses contain DNA—the very genetic instructions of life? Surely God designed the chemical code that brings both life and death. If God is stimulating the cosmos to increasingly complex forms of order, it seems apparent that this complexity is also producing devastating diseases and increased suffering. Why are there monstrous people whose actions cannot easily and logically be explained by looking at past generations? What evidence is there that the world is moving toward universal harmony? For me, there are still too many loose ends and unanswered questions in the process answer.

The theologies of dualism, privation, and process all provide explanations that Christians have found helpful. Theories about evil, however, are probably less important than the spiritual resources that Christian folk have developed to cope with suffering. The bottom line is that no matter "why" it is that evil exists, suffering is present in human life and allowed to operate. No one position seems to provide answers that satisfy all my questions.

Powerlessness and Crisis

Human relationships are often as knotted as Alzheimer's neurofibrillary tangles. R. D. Laing brilliantly captures these relational knots in the following couplets about suffering:

> He can't be happy
>   when there is so much suffering in the world
> She can't be happy
>   if he is unhappy

She wants to be happy
He does not feel entitled to be happy

She wants him to be happy
and he wants her to be happy

He feels guilty if he is happy
and guilty if she is not happy

She wants both to be happy
He wants her to be happy

So they are both unhappy.[22]

Laing traces familiar patterns of human suffering in what he calls "webs of *maya*," that is, webs of illusion. Tangled, knotty relationships lead to the overwhelming experiences that cause emotional and spiritual crises. At one time, I felt locked into a tangled relationship. My anger and powerlessness led to these lines:

Sometimes I am so
afraid you will
never commit
yourself to me I
dig me a trench
pile the dirt on my
head and spit it
out at the world.

The working definition of a "crisis" used by the Office of Ministries with Women in Crisis is a useful one for us to consider:

A crisis occurs when a woman finds life's experiences overwhelming. As a result, she is locked into unwanted situations which she cannot escape, and she faces problems which she cannot solve with her usual resources.[23]

A human crisis also occurs when institutions with authority produce conditions that citizens are powerless to correct. Two current examples will make the point.

---

[22] R. D. Laing, *Knots* (New York: Vintage Books, 1970), p. 27. Copyright © 1970 by R. D. Laing. Reprinted by permission of Pantheon Books, a division of Random House. Used by permission.

[23] Coppernoll and Halsey, *Crisis*, p. 1.

The U.S. Department of Health and Human Services is planning to build 2,900 new homes for Native Americans—*without indoor plumbing*. Officials of the Indian Health Service reported that 20,000 homes already occupied by Native Americans are without indoor plumbing. The Occupational Safety and Health Administration of the U.S. government has decided not to force growers to provide drinking water and toilets for the 500,000 farm workers in the United States. Two outside consultants testified that thousands of farm workers already suffer from parasitic illnesses as well as hepatitis and dysentery.[24] These are the same laborers who work long hours for little pay to bring fresh fruits and vegetables to your supermarket at reasonable prices.

Can you imagine the outrage if the federal government tried to do the same thing to middle-class people? These actions imply that Native Americans and farm laborers are not entitled to the human comforts that the rest of the United States enjoys. Evidently it is just fine for "Indians" and migrants to use outhouses or the fields and ditches as their toilets.

Native Americans and migrant laborers are locked into an unwanted situation from which they cannot escape and in which they cannot solve with their own resources. They are powerless before decisions of the mighty federal government. Thinkers in the field of social justice would call the plight of the Native Americans and migrant laborers evidence of "systemic" evil. Systemic evil means that the suffering is caused by an unjust "system."

When experiences seem overwhelming and not solvable, no matter what the problem may be, the sufferer feels powerless. The feeling that life is out of control can lead to symptoms of anxiety, depression—even suicidal despair. The Christian community gives the assurance, however, that no matter how tragic the circumstances—whether because of "the quirky mass of imperfections" in nature or because of human forces that attempt to kill the human spirit—suffering can be redeemed.

---

[24] Both examples are included in "For the Record," *Sojourners*, June, 1985, p. 13.

To assert that suffering may be "redeemed" is to express the conviction that pain need not necessarily be a destructive force in human lives. Suffering is never denied or forgotten, but misery is not the final chapter either. Not only can the sufferer recover the equilibrium once known but can go on to become a stronger self.

Christians are not powerless before hostile forces. The Bible teaches that God's people are no longer powerless (Colossians 2). Christ, the resurrected one, empowers believers. Paul writes to the Corinthians:

> Then you will have the proof you seek of the Christ who speaks through me, the Christ who, far from being weak with you, *makes his power felt among you*. True, he died on the cross in weakness, but he lives by the power of God; and we who share his weakness shall by the power of God live with him in your service (II Corinthians 13:3-4).

Therefore, the Bible counsels us that when we are overwhelmed and feeling powerless, we should:

> Be rooted in Jesus.
> Be built in Jesus.
> Be established in the faith [we] were taught.
> (Colossians 2:7)

We are not powerless, testifies the New Testament. Nevertheless, in order to cope with suffering, we need a good dose of Christian realism. Sometimes there is simply no way to transcend the limits of our genetic inheritance or to change the psychological relationships that have formed our lives. It will also help to eliminate any simple romanticism about nature. And we need to battle our natural indifference over the human predators who roam the earth. In spite of crisis and adversity, and when we're burdened, heavy laden, we *can learn* to sing, *"Hallelujah Anyhow!"*

Weaving New Life from Tangles: Stories of Courage

Christianity does not deny pain. Physical pain is an event that happens naturally when something threatens to damage our bodies. It is a mistake to underestimate the extent to which physical pain itself can wound the soul. Continued and intense physical pain is not particularly ennobling. Pain is not to be transcended but relieved by all medical or psychological means.

The sufferer's inner attitude, however, exercises a powerful effect on how one copes with the experience of pain. Too many Americans use drugs at the least uncomfortable twinge of either physical or psychic pain. Rather, persons with strong, vital personalities in normal good health will not permit physical pain to take up too much room in their consciousness or their conversations.[25]

We admire those persons whose positive inner attitude toward constant pain has had a transformative effect on their lives. My friend Elizabeth Cook, who lives at The Hermitage in Northern Virginia (a United Methodist retirement community), has suffered through thirty-seven serious operations during her life and now fights crippling rheumatoid arthritis. Elizabeth seldom complains. Out of curiosity, I asked her if she had pain in her feet. "Oh yes," she exclaimed, "some mornings the pain is so strong I am not certain I can walk." On those mornings, Elizabeth explained, she talks to her feet, saying, "Come on feet. You and I are friends, and we must work together—so it is time to get moving." Elizabeth keeps walking, smiling, and helping others who live in her community.

Elizabeth Cook faces the unwelcome disease, enters into the experience and "befriends" her suffering feet. She does not glorify or build her life around the pain. Elizabeth describes her faith as very "simple"— she trusts God to be present, helping her to endure and giving her the power to transform the pain into personal strength.

Ludwig van Beethoven reacted differently to suffering. A life-mask of the master composer dated 1812 shows him as scowling and miserable, condemned to deafness and chronic ill health.[26] Beethoven had become aware of his

---

[25]Ferdinand Sauerbruch and Hans Wenke, *Pain: Its Meaning and Significance*, trans. by Edward Fitzgerald (London: Allen & Unwin Ltd., 1963), p. 20.

[26]All quotations and information about Beethoven are taken from R. M. James, *Beethoven* (London: Evergreen Lives, 1983). Used by permission of St. Martin's Press, Inc., New York.

growing deafness from the earliest days of his musical fame and, at that time, still in his youth, he said: "I will take Fate by the throat!" Fate, however, was not kind. By age thirty, he wrote to a friend, "My ears buzz and hum day and night." Two years later, he wrote:

> From year to year my hopes of being cured have gradually been shattered, and finally I have been forced to accept the prospect of a permanent infirmity. . . . If I appear in company I am overcome by a burning anxiety, a fear that I am running the risk of letting people know of my condition. How humiliated I have felt if someone standing beside me heard the sound of a flute in the distance and I heard nothing, or if somebody heard a shepherd sing and again I heard nothing. Such experiences almost made me despair, and I was on the point of putting an end to my life. The only thing that held me back was my art. For indeed it seemed impossible to leave this world before I had produced all the works that I felt the urge to compose; and thus I have dragged on this miserable existence.[27]

Beethoven had been the most brilliant pianist of his age. Now he could not even hear the music he continued to compose. Alternately he raged against his fate or lived in quiet desperation. As the deafness progressed, Beethoven withdrew from society and lived in virtual isolation. He seemed to "act out" his despair and cultivated a grubby and dishevelled appearance. His apartment was described as disorderly. Most of the chairs were "decorated with clothes and with dishes full of the remains of the previous day's supper." Beethoven increasingly was driven into an inner solitude. Only music seemed to support and sustain him.

It is an awesome fact that, in spite of these outer manifestations of depression, Beethoven's music became more powerful and innovative the deafer he grew. The *Missa Solemnis*, his "spiritual testament," is surely some of the greatest music ever composed using the traditional texts for Holy Communion. Along with the *Ninth Symphony* and the *Grosse Fugue*, it was written when he was totally deaf.

Beethoven appeared to be "driven." Biographer R. M.

---

[27]Beethoven wrote what he thought would be his last will and testament at age thirty-two in the town of Heiligenstadt, Austria. The *Heiligenstadt Testament* was intended for his brothers, Carl and Johann.

James says that he worked at fever-pitch to compose his greatest achievement, the *Ninth Symphony*. The first performance was on 7 May 1824. When it was over, the hall erupted in a frenzy of applause. In what must have been one of the saddest events in the history of music, as the applause swelled, one of the soloists noticed the stone-deaf Beethoven still standing with his head bowed, back to the audience whose cheers he could not hear. She turned him around; only then did he realize what he had achieved.

A still-tormented Beethoven died on 26 March 1827 when he was fifty-six years old. At five o'clock in the afternoon, during a thunderstorm, a loud clap of thunder filled the air and a bolt of lightening illuminated the room. A friend who was present wrote that the dying Beethoven opened his eyes, raised his right hand, and looked upward for several seconds with his fist clenched and with a threatening expression which seemed to say, "I defy you, powers of evil! God is with me. . . ." His hand sunk to the bed and he stopped breathing. More than 20,000 people thronged to the funeral. His grave stone was erected with the one word, "BEETHOVEN."

Beethoven's religious faith was complex, unorthodox and profound. It reminds me of a stanza in a poem by Rainer Maria Rilke:

> Yet no matter how deeply I go down into myself
> my God is dark, and like a webbing made of
> a hundred roots, that drink in silence.[28]

The true stories of Elizabeth Cook and Ludwig van Beethoven show very different ways of handling suffering. Yet, neither person was powerless. Their stories indicate that suffering is not morally pointless. In a marvelous book containing victorious stories of persons dying of cancer, Elizabeth Kubler-Ross writes:

> In the course of a terminal illness, we can give up, we can demand attention, we can scream, we can become total invalids long before it is necessary. . . . Or we have the choice to complete our work, to funtion in whatever way we are capable and

---

[28]*Selected Poems of Rainer Maria Rilke*, trans. Robert Bly (New York: Harper & Row Publishers, 1981), p. 15.

thereby touch many lives by our valiant struggle and our own sense of purpose in our own existence.[29]

The energy created by suffering may lead to a life devoted to charity or to writing eternally great music. There are as many different paths to handling suffering positively as there are people who suffer; what follows is but one of those paths.[30]

Path to Power

First: Name the Pain

A flight from suffering characterizes the practice of many western Christians. Americans tend to look for magical cures for their problems. Medical practitioners, both physicians and psychiatrists, become secular saviours. Many who suffer hope that one more valium or one more drink will numb the pain.

The final report of a crisis survey of United Methodists revealed that one out of every thirty respondents had been raped and one in every nine had known a family member or close friend who had been raped. The report concluded, however, that "denial runs deep," and "we encountered disbelief and an amazing capacity to rationalize the findings.[31] Denial is not usually productive. Christians must accept pain and name its cause honestly for themselves and before God.

The healing power of God is ever-present and Christians should not be afraid of honestly naming the source of their pain. Believers have a very important role in helping God redeem suffering by acknowledging the nature of the deep wounds that engulf and threaten to overwhelm.

---

[29]Elizabeth Kubler-Ross, *To Live Until We Say Goodby* (Englewood Cliffs, New Jersey: Prentice-Hall, Inc., 1978), p. 14.

[30]Readers will recognize these suggestions as influenced by the *via negativa*, as interpreted in the "letting go and letting be" spiritual tradition of Meister Eckhart (1260-c.1329) and the current revival of "creation spirituality" by Matthew Fox, *Original Blessing* (Santa Fe, New Mexico: Bear & Company, 1983), pp. 132-157.

[31]Coppernoll and Halsey, *Crisis*, p. 3.

Second: Enter Suffering and Let It Go

Christianity began as a religion of marginal people, that is, those folk who lived on the edges or fringes of power in the Roman empire. Membership included a large membership of slaves, the poor and wealthy women. It was not possible for the earliest Christians to avoid or flee from suffering. No wonder the Church saw power in the mystery of the cross. The Christian acceptance of suffering, however, does not mean passive tranquility.[32]

A friend passed on an important piece of wisdom to me when I was battling with anxiety. The panic attacks came upon me like waves and I fought against their coming. The friend counseled me "to go with the waves." Anxiety about having anxiety produced a snowballing effect which compounded the suffering. I learned to "go with the waves," abandoning myself and entering into the breakers. In one sense, I "befriended" the waves when finally I politely thanked my body for the message of danger but assured myself that I was going on anyway. In a similar way, Elizabeth Cook calls her painful, uncooperative feet "her friends" and commands them to move.

When a sufferer is able to enter into the pain and let it be pain, without glorifying or wallowing in it, then spiritual healing may break through. By God's grace, the struggle can become "fuel" for our journey. To "let the pain go" does not mean the sharp physical sensations, emotional grief, or the anger caused by oppressive circumstances will quickly "go away." To let the pain go means that we no longer let suffering itself be the force that dominates our lives.

Very often "letting go" means forgiving one's self or another for real or imagined wrongs. The church has always affirmed that confession may provide the occasion for healing. The process of "naming," "entering," and "letting go" is as valid for the suffering caused by broken relationships as it is for the physical manifestations of a disease.

Third: Witness to the Power

John Hick in his classical study, *Evil and the God of Love,*

---

[32]Dorothee Soelle, *Suffering*, trans. Everett R. Kalin (Philadelphia: Fortress Press, 1975), pp. 101-108.

believes that God created this world as "a place for soul making."[33] If we don't push Hick's idea to the extreme (that is, we certainly do not want to say that God intentionally created suffering to produce good character), the concept of "soul making" may be a helpful image.[34] A more traditional way to speak of this process is called "sanctification."

Sanctification comes from the Latin word *sanctus* which means "holy" or "consecrated." To sanctify means to be made holy. The church has always been in general agreement that it is only by God's gracious presence that a believer participates in the ongoing process of being sanctified. A great family quarrel erupted, however, during the sixteenth century over the issue of how much importance should be given to good deeds in the sanctifying process.

Protestant Reformers were afraid that ordinary Christians, looking to the holiness of the saints, would decide that such a life of good works brought with it earned merit and forgiveness of sins. They declared, quite rightly, that the people of God should never zealously copy the lives of holy people in order to earn righteousness. We become righteous or holy before God only because of our faith in the work of Christ, the mediator and reconciler.[35] The fact that some Christians are still suspicious of the term "saints" stems from this controversy.

All branches of Methodism look to John Wesley for an interpretation of sanctification.[36] Wesley was convinced that God's gracious initiative calls forth a human response in both personal salvation and social transformation. Preven-

---

[33]John Hick follows Irenaeus and Origen in his views.

[34]The image is not intended to imply a split between body and spirit. Most western psychology believes that physical and spiritual realities are a unified whole. The older metaphor of soul-making points toward the spiritual growth that is possible for each person.

[35]The Protestant doctrine of Justification by Faith is classically stated in Article XX of *The Augsburg Confession* of 1530 and in Article IV of *The Apology of the Augsburg Confession* in *The Book of Concord, The Confessions of the Evangelical Lutheran Church*, Theodore G. Tappert, transl. & ed. (Philadelphia: Fortress Press, 1959).

[36]Thomas A. Langford, *Practical Divinity, Theology in the Wesleyan Tradition* (Nashville: Abingdon Press, 1983) and *The Future of the Methodist Theological Traditions*, M. Douglas Meeks, ed. (Nashville: Abingdon Press, 1985).

ient grace—that is, God's gift that goes before human action, opens the way to a new quality of human life. While Christian sanctity is a gift of grace and not an achievement, Wesley, nevertheless, was very optimistic about its reality in redeemed lives. He even dared to speak of the "perfect" love of God and neighbor as the ultimate goal of Christian discipleship. Growth in holiness is gradual and progressive through the transforming power of the Holy Spirit. Wesley found evidence for Christian perfection in the biographies of saintly people. Two "saints" that he particularly admired were Gregory Lopez and Brother Lawrence.

Gregory Lopez (1542-96) was a page in the court of Philip II of Spain in his youth. A religious experience at the shrine of Our Lady of Guadalupe in Spain led him on a pilgrimage to Mexico. In Mexico he sold his considerable possessions and gave the proceeds to the poor of Vera Cruz. In 1589 he built a hermitage with a friend and devoted the rest of his life to prayer, scripture study and helping the poor.[37] Brother Lawrence (1611-1691), whose real name was Nicholas Herman, was a lay brother assigned to kitchen duties in a Carmelite monastery in Paris. He left a journal on "the practice of the presence of God" during his forty years among the pots and pans of the kitchen. God's presence gave him such total joy that word spread about his life throughout the French church. Brother Lawrence declared that he was as aware of God's grace "within the noise and clatter of my kitchen . . . as if I were upon knees at the blessed sacrament.[38]

United Methodists should be quite at home with a concept of "soul making." Our tradition has a historical bias toward accenting the transforming power of God which leads to growth in holiness. We believe that the gospel claims the necessity and possibility for a sanctified way of life—a life of profound personal and prophetic courage.

Why Do Bad Things Happen to Good People?

Why do bad things happen to good people? Why do good

---

[37]John J. Delaney, *Dictionary of Saints* (Garden City, New York: Doubleday & Company, Inc., 1980), p. 363.

[38]Elliott Wright, *Holy Company, Christian Heroes and Heroines* (New York: Macmillan Publishing Co., Inc., 1980), p. 85.

things happen to bad people?[39] I honestly don't know. In a sense these are not my questions. Jesus accepted the existence of the devil and regarded evil as an inevitable part of creation. He did not offer an explanation for the existence of evil or of its final destiny. I cannot locate evil so precisely in a personality such as Satan. But, like Jesus, I acknowledge that evil is an important fact—not to be denied or explained away. For me, the reason that suffering exists in the created order is a mystery. What I do know for certain, for good or for ill, is that this is the world we have been given and in this world, suffering is undeniable and unavoidable.

Beauty, laughter and much pleasure are also to be found on this planet. There *is* meaning and purpose in living. I trust the biblical promises that God is present in the greatest joy, the most extreme suffering and in all stages in between. The potential for a deepened spiritual life, that is, for soul making, exists because Chritians have faith that the healing power of God in Christ works for our benefit. Spiritual help *is* available, empowering and enabling the sufferer to weave a new cloth for living out of the tangled threads of existence.

A future is possible for those who suffer. Pain is not the final word. Sanctification, by the power of the Holy Spirit, is an ongoing process of life. The living witness of true, honest stories from the community of faith is an essential ingredient in learning Christian courage. The Church lives victoriously by moving from memory to hope. As J. Philip Wogaman suggests, Christians belong to a "community of hopeful love."[40] We remember the testimony of God's deliverance through the record of scripture and tradition, in the history we proclaim and teach, and in the story sign-actions we celebrate in the sacraments. Remembering what God has done in the past, and believing in the testimony of the "saints," we are able to trust that the promises of God will be fulfilled even in our own lives. Today!

---

[39]In a very honest and direct way, Psalm 73 asks why the wicked prosper and the righteous suffer? Psalm 77 cries, "Is God's right arm powerless to act?" Remembering the mighty deeds of God in the past strengthens both psalmists in their present crisis.

[40] J. Philip Wogaman, *Faith and Fragmentation,* p. 147.

Prayer of the Church

O God, the source of all health: So fill our hearts with faith in your love, that with calm expectancy we may make room for your power to possess us, and gracefully accept your healing; through Jesus Christ our Lord.[41]

Discussion Questions

1. What were you taught about sin and evil as a child? Were any of the explanations given to you described in this chapter? Do you still believe what you were taught or have you adopted a new explanation?

2. The content of this chapter returns to questions of theodicy. How does the author answer the question (here and throughout the book), "why do bad things happen to good people?"

3. R. D. Laing's poetic whirligig points to the tangled nature of destructive relationships. How could living through the steps of "naming the pain," "entering into" and "letting go of the suffering," help solve relational problems before they reach the crisis stage?

4. The author claims that the structural violence of systems, for example, unjust governmental decisions may bring about terrible consequences for human beings. In what ways may Christians work to remove the evil of structural violence? Share personal stories of structural suffering. Do you think it is possible to redeem these situations?

5. What do you think makes the difference between lives that are *destroyed* by suffering and the new lives that are *forged* by suffering? Can you think of examples of both situations?

---

[41] Written by John W. Sutter, *The Book of Common Prayer*, p. 46.

Spiritual Exercises

Spiritual Exercise I: Hymn to Joy

Beethoven's triumphant *Ninth Symphony* was written when he was completely deaf. He chose to compose the music to compliment a poem that he admired. Schiller's "Ode to Joy" was a poem in praise of universal friendship. It provided Beethoven with the magnificent fourth-movement finale written for chorus and orchestra.

If you have access to a recording of the *Ninth Symphony*, by all means play the choral finale for your group. If you cannot listen to the actual orchestral work, you can still hear the tune that Beethoven composed to Schiller's "Ode to Joy" by playing "Joyful, Joyful, We Adore Thee," number 38 in *The Book of Hymns*. The words are not Schiller's, however, but come from the poetry of Henry van Dyke.

While you listen to "Hymn to Joy," think about the life of Beethoven. The leader might ask the following questions as a guided meditation:

1. How would you feel if your ears started to "buzz and hum day and night?"

2. Suppose you went to the doctor and were told that you were going deaf?

3. Would you be afraid, as was Beethoven, of letting people know about your condition? What if you knew it would slowly affect your job?

4. How do you account for Beethoven's creativity even while he suffered the agony of deafness?

5. Beethoven's music kept him going on with life. What kinds of things would keep you going? How could your faith help sustain you through such a crisis?

Spiritual Exercise II: Imaging Your Journey

Every person has times that hurt and times that heal. It is good to recall these low points in relationship to other healing experiences in your life. Considering the natural progress of both pain and promise together may enable you to see your journey in a new way.

109

A life-journey can be visualized in a number of ways. Anthea Francine, the founder of *Women's Quest*, suggests that the ancient image of the spiral is an especially appropriate symbol to represent a woman's journey. Francine thinks that this concept is beautifully illustrated by the living sea shell of the nautilus.

The shell of the nautilus is made up of many dividing skeletal walls which become entrance points for a new section of the sea creature. Like the shell of the nautilus, human lives are filled with passages where persons lurch and launch into a new relationship with self and environment.[42] You may want to think about the times that hurt and heal in connection with the image of the nautilus.

Reflect on Your Journey Using a Timeline

Another way to map your life journey is by recording the events that hurt and healed along a timeline. Here is a process for using a time line:

1. Create mental images for the points of hurt and healing in your journey. Remember the work you did with images in Chapter 1.
2. Draw a line across a blank sheet of paper. Use only symbols to depict your journey.
3. Complete the diagram by recording the year each event occurred on top of the image.
4. Draw up a code for your symbols.
5. Share what you feel comfortable revealing with the group.

Standing on the Promises of God

A good conclusion for your study of "Tangles" might be to sing or read together "Standing on the Promises," # 221 in *The Book of Hymns*.

---

[42] Anthea Francine can be contacted at *Women's Quest*, 2828 Cherry Street, Berkeley, California, 94705.

Further Reading

Some Reading for Children

Children suffer the same as adults and they deserve their own "canonical stories." Two helpful books for parents that contain usable stories for children are: Anderson, Peggy *Children's Hospital*. New York: Harper & Row, 1985, and Jampolsky, Gerald G. *There is a Rainbow Behind Every Dark Cloud*. Tiburon, California (19 Main Street, 94920): The Center for Attitudinal Healing, 1978.

James, Howe. *The Hospital Book*. New York: Crown Publishers, Inc., 1981. What to expect when going to the hospital.

Kesselman, Wendy. *Emma*. New York: Harper Trophy Book, Harper & Row Publishers, 1980. *Emma* is the story of a seventy-two year old woman who takes up painting.

Peterson, Jeanne Whitehouse. *I Have a Sister Who Is Deaf*. New York: Harper & Row, 1977. A young child lovingly describes her sister.

Wittman, Sally, *A Special Trade*. New York: Harper Trophy Book, Harper & Row Publisher, 1978. Nelly helps an older neighbor, Bartholomew, when he returns from the hospital in a wheelchair.

Further Reading for Adults

Dobihal, Edward F. and Stewart, Charles William. *When a Friend is Dying, A Guide to Caring for the Terminally Ill and Bereaved*. Nashville: Abingdon, 1984.

Fox, Matthew, *Original Blessing*. Santa Fe, New Mexico: Bear & Company, 1983.

Kubler-Ross, Elizabeth. *To Live Until We Say Goodby*. Englewood Cliffs, New Jersey: Prentice-Hall, Inc., 1978.

Sanford, John A. *Evil, The Shadow Side of Reality*. New York: The Crossroad Publishing Company, 1981.

Soelle, Dorothee. *Suffering*, trans. Everett R. Kalin. Philadelphia: Fortress Press, 1975.

Watts, Alan W. *The Two Hands of God, The Myths of Polarity*. New York: Collier Books, 1963. Legends of good and evil from Chinese, Indian, Egyptian, Iranian, and early Christian civilizations.

Wogaman, J. Philip. *Faith and Fragmentation, Christianity for a New Age*. Philadelphia: Fortress Press, 1985.

CONCLUSION

CHAPTER VI

JOURNEY TOWARD WHOLENESS

Heal me, O Lord and I shall be healed,
save me and I shall be saved;
for thou art my praise.
(Jeremiah 17:14, NEB)

We are on a journey toward wholeness—a journey of "becoming." Traveling bodily about life, clothed by our skin, energized by a pumping heart, and nourished by experiences and symbols that are transmitted to a complex brain, we yearn for *shalom*. We long to make the same affirmation of God's goodness to our traveling body-spirit as did fourteenth-century anchoress Julian of Norwich, who exclaimed: "I saw that God is everything that is good and energizing. God is our clothing that wraps, clasps and encloses us so as to never leave us."[1]

Shalom expresses God's purpose for all living beings. This Hebrew word is often translated into English as "peace," but it means much more than the absence of conflict. *Shalom* is being in harmony with one's self and with all creation. *Shalom* means commitment to living in community with neighbor and world. We seek a unity of being in which body and spirit are in a state of comfortableness with self and environment. Experiencing the unity and well-being of *shalom* is a joy that may cause a spontaneous dance. In the *Peanuts* cartoon strip by Charles Schultz, when Snoopy the dog feels especially free and "all-together" he does a "helicopter dance"—that is, Snoopy swirls and whirls until

---

[1] *Meditations with Julian of Norwich*, Brendan Doyle, ed. (Sante Fe, New Mexico: Bear and Company, 1983), p. 24. An "anchoress" was a Christian woman who vowed to live alone and apart from medieval society for the purpose of prayer and meditation.

his long Beagle ears look like a rotating propeller. Over seven hundred years before there was a Snoopy, a Christian Beguine laywoman, Mechtild of Magdeburg wrote:

Leap!
    Leap in ordered dance—
        Be a vanquisher
            of evil spirits![2]

The biblical witness confirms the suspicion that there are not one but rather two ways to be pulled in our journey: (1) toward wholeness and *shalom*, or (2) toward fragmentation and self-destruction. In the midst of an unfinished painful world a person can refuse to endure. We may elect to bear our pains heavily and give up hope. The sin of despair or loss of hope is an ultimate temptation.[3]

During this study on suffering, we have listened to many personal stories of individuals who have chosen to name their pain and, by looking honestly at its cause, have channeled their energies in creative and healing directions. They have discovered, as did Mechtild in the thirteenth century, that God's promise is true: "When your Easter comes, I shall be all around you, I shall be through and through you."[4]

The Christian community affirms that no matter what temptations pull us toward self-destruction, God cease-lessly pulls us toward healing, toward *shalom*. Christians call this activity the work of the Holy Spirit. The transforming power of the Spirit has been given to the community of faith—to the church. Through the ministry of the church, we learn that believers can connect into the power of the Spirit. We also learn that *shalom* is God's intention for our world. The church teaches us that a vision of peace, justice and well-being are at the very heart of the story of God's continuing revelation.

---

[2] *Meditations with Mechtild of Magdeburg,* Sue Woodruff, ed. (Santa Fe, New Mexico: Bear & Company, 1982), p. 95. Beguines were women of the lower classes who lived together and worked for a living but did not become nuns and did not marry.

[3] See Julian of Norwich, *Meditations,* p. 121.

[4] *Meditations with Mechtild of Magdeburg,* p. 95.

The Christian Community Has a Story

The Christian community has its own story to tell. The church is the bearer of the story for the community of faith. The biblical narrative provides the foundational material. Theologian George A. Lindbeck believes that to be a Christian "is to learn the story of Israel and of Jesus well enough to interpret and experience oneself and one's world in its terms."[5]

In communicating the biblical material, the teller (the church) develops an ongoing tradition. Rich and varied in content, the continuing story of faith comes from different regions of the world and has accumulated over a long period of time. We call this expanded report "the tradition," although it is probably more accurate to speak of "traditions." The faith stories of individual believers, you and me, are a growing part of the continual stream that combine to make up *the* Christian Story.

What keeps the Christian community telling the old, old stories of faith from the Bible—and newer ones too? Stories of suffering and redemption are remembered because healing power is to be found in the listening and telling. The Passover festival for Jews recollects the misery of slavery and the escape from bondage. Passover reminds Jews of their continued identity as a covenant people. The Cherokees tell their children about the horrors of the "trail of tears" so that, in remembering their past, they may be energized for present struggles. Poet Alice Walker reflects on a monument of a stone eagle erected in Georgia by the Cherokees:[6]

> Pinned to the earth
> The eagle endures
> The Cherokees are gone
> The people come on tours.
> And on surrounding National
> Forest lakes the air rings
> With cries
> The silenced make.

---

[5] George A. Lindbeck, *The Nature of Doctrine, Religion and Theology in a Postliberal Age* (Philadelphia: The Westminster Press, 1984), p. 34.

[6] Alice Walker, from "Eagle Rock" in *Revolutionary Petunias & Other Poems.* (New York: Harcourt Brace Javonovich, Inc., 1973), p. 21. Used by permission.

The Cherokees will not be silenced as long as they continue to pass the history of their struggles along to new generations. Communities tell stories of suffering in order to do as artist Kenji Mayazawa advises: Go straight into the suffering and "burn all struggle as your fuel."[7] Be energized, he suggests, by using the struggle as fuel for courage. The Christian community tells its particular story of crucifixion and resurrection for the same reason. The faith story of the church assists in understanding and interpreting the world as believers internalize and adopt it as their own story. The struggle and promise of the tradition then becomes the fuel to deal with personal crises.

George A. Lindbeck believes that the Christian story provides a framework that shapes a believer's life and thought. The story is a communal reality. Religion is not primarily a set of propositions to be believed, he claims, "but is rather the medium in which one moves, a set of skills that one employs in living one's life."[8] The ritual enactment of the church's story in word and sacraments contains religious power that promotes a real transformation of character.

A sudden calamity can halt a feeling of well-being. Being victimized and powerless retards inner peace, but in the midst of doubt there is "good news." The story told in the Christian community communicates the promise that suffering can be redeemed. The cross was not the final chapter. "O Death where is thy victory? O Death where is thy sting?" shouted the early church. Victory is won! Jesus is raised!

Remembering into the Future[9]

Spiritual power is present in the community of faith to help believers cope with suffering. When the faithful participate in the Christian story, we are *remembering into the future.* The living memory of the tradition, through ritual

[7] Fox, *Compassion,* p. 120.

[8] Lindbeck, *The Nature of Doctrine,* p. 35.

[9] "Remembering into the Future" was the theme of the annual convention of the National Association of Pastoral Musicians in 1983.

action, music and prayer shapes our response to the present and prepares us to live faithfully, whatever happens in the future. We are challenged to become a just and holy people by remembering the religious events that have formed our faith.

There are many ways through which the community of faith heals by remembering into the future. The ritual action of our worship, that is, the images found in word, music, prayer and in the sacramental signs of water, bread and wine stir our imaginations and prepare us for living the way of *shalom*. The symbolic language of our faith provides images that give us courage and hope.[10]

Using positive religious imagery can help alter feelings of hopelessness. Persons who are able mentally to picture *the cause* of their pain and image ways *to gain power* over the suffering have learned an effective skill to cope with feelings of helplessness. Mental imaging involves highly personal and symbolic language. The story of the Christian faith provides many healing signs that can strengthen and empower the believer:

Religious visions from the past
　that are allowed to inform a present problem
　　help to construct and shape a new future.

Physicians have discovered the power of using positive mental imagery to influence healing in the body. By drawing the mental pictures of their disease on paper, cancer patients have decreased their fears and brought about attitudinal changes that have restored their will to live. Claims have been made that the ability to visualize recovery has actually strengthened the immune system that fights the cancer cells.[11] Positive mental imagery can also serve to decrease tension and stress.

Relaxation and mental imagery are among the most

---

[10] For a good discussion on this point see John H. Westerhoff III, *Living the Faith Community, the Church that Makes a Difference* (Minneapolis; Winston Press, 1985).

[11] O. Carl Simonton, Stephanie Matthews-Simonton and James L. Creighton, *Getting Well Again* (New York: Bantam Books, 1978), chapters 11 and 12.

valuable tools in helping persons learn to believe in their own ability to cope with and to transform suffering.[12] Learning the skill of picture-imagery is easy. It can be done individually or in a group. These are the steps in the process. Always allow yourself or the group time to center and relax before creating mental images.

1. First, *think out a mental picture of your suffering*. The image could come from physical pain, a disease, a deteriorating relationship or perhaps a personal characteristic (guilt, anger) that you would like to change.

2. Next, *draw a simple picture* that represents what you believe causes your suffering. For example, stick figures, line drawings or cartoon images are fine. It is important to record the image on paper so that you can remember and reflect on it later.

3. Now, *focus on a healing image from the Bible*. The biblical image should be one that will reinforce your will to resist the suffering. Remembering your religious heritage will encourage you to stand firm before hostile forces. Here are two types of biblical symbols:

a. Many empowering images are found in the Psalms. Here are some of my favorites taken from the NEB translation. If one of these metaphors seems to strike a responsive cord, add it to your picture by means of a simple line drawing.

"God is our shelter and our refuge" (Psalm 46:1).

"God stamps out war, . . . breaks the bow, . . . snaps the spear, . . . and burns the shield. . ." (Psalm 46:9).

"When the earth rocks, with all who live on it, I make the pillars firm" (Psalm 75:3).

"I will take refuge in the shadow of thy wings until the storms are past" (Psalm 57:1).

"The mountains melt like wax as the LORD approaches . . ." (Psalm 97:5).

"The LORD nurses him on his sick-bed;
   and turns his bed when he is ill" (Psalm 41:3).

"Now I will lie down in peace, and sleep;

---

[12] There are many useful books and tapes on the techniques of relaxation. Simonton, *Getting Well Again,* chapter 11, contains a good summary of this skill.

for thou alone, O Lᴏʀᴅ, makest me live unafraid"
(Psalm 4:8).

"Thou hast given me the shield of my salvation, thy hand
sustains me, thy providence makes me great,

Thou givest me room for my steps, my feet have not
faltered" (Psalm 18:35-36).

"The Lᴏʀᴅ is my light and my salvation;

whom shall I fear?" (Psalm 27:1).

b. Annie Vallotton is the Swiss teacher who created the
wonderful line drawings used by the American Bible
Society in the Today's English Version (*Good News Bible*).
The simplicity and honesty of these line drawings invites
the reader to participate in the meaning of the story of faith
told in the Bible. Annie Vallotton's drawings, or your own
version of scripture stories, may be added to the symbolic
picture you are drawing.[13]

4. *Add a positive sign from the scriptures to your picture image.*
Pick one of these strengthening biblical images, or another
that is a favorite, and add it to your picture. Below is a
sample of a picture-image I did while trying to control my
weight. Food and fluids are pictured in this image as being

LIGHT RAYS FROM THE
POWER OF CHRIST

HOLY MEAL

MS. FAT CELLS

---

[13] Annie Vallotton published 192 line drawings in the *Today's English
Version (TEV)* for the American Bible Society. At a reasonable cost, a teacher
can show these scripture drawings to the group. The American Bible
Society, P.O. Box 5656, Grand Central Station, New York, New York,
10017, has a set of Vallotton drawings on posters. For a nominal cost,
Griggs Educational Service, 1731 Barcelona Street, Livermore, California
94550, has packets of twenty different cards of Vallotton's line drawings.

Donald L. Griggs has suggested in his workbook, *Translating the Good
News through Teaching Activities,* (Nashville: Abingdon, 1980), that a leader
may also purchase a large print edition of the TEV from the American Bible
Society (a New Testament costs $1.50, #02850), cut out the line drawings
and mount them on blank file cards. Or Griggs suggests that you could
transfer the line drawings onto transparencies and project them with an
overhead projector.

consumed by Ms. Pacwoman fat cells.[14] No matter how much I dieted, the fat cells got larger and larger. Images from the community of faith helped at two levels. I imagined the light of Christ reaching into my body with its healing warmth. The holy communion meal of bread and wine strengthened my real need for spiritual food and encouraged me not to reward or punish myself with unhealthy eating habits.

5. Finally, *imagine yourself healthy and free from suffering.* Pat yourself mentally on the back for participating in your empowerment. Be assured that positive mental imagery works for your benefit. The symbols of the community of faith encourage us in the journey of life. We remember into the past record of our faith in order to be strengthened for tomorrow's tasks.

The Healing Ministry of the Community of Faith

The Christian story centers around the reality of resurrection. The healing ministry of the church is a powerful sign of this new life. The Christian is called to witness of this saving faith to friends and neighbors. A person who has deeply suffered often becomes acutely conscious of the suffering of others. We need to be aware that we can pass on our power and become a source for healing. For example, a widow who has worked through the pain of death will try to help another with a recent loss. One widow's sorrow thus links with another's sadness. She can testify to the power that gave her the strength to endure and the victory woven from the tangles of broken dreams.

The young daughter of my friends, Judy and Bruce Birch, died on her third birthday of acute lymphocytic leukemia. Bruce writes of the sustaining witness of the Christian community in Kansas and South Carolina and concludes that there seem to be three roles for the church during such crises. First, the Christian community can help to relieve the isolation and terrible sense of loneliness that comes in the

---

[14] The image of Ms. Pacwoman is taken from the video game of similar name.

midst of such hardships. Second, the congregation should hold up symbols of the faith—such as the meaning of the stories of Exodus and resurrection, as a way of seeing "God's gift of life even beyond the offense of the moment." Finally, the community of faith mediates for the future when it refuses to let the pain of loss constitute the final word.[15]

Julian of Norwich, a fourteenth-century anchoress, believed that pain produced "a great *oneing* between Christ and us."[16] In his solidarity with the sufferer, Jesus asked those he healed, "Do you want to be made whole?" The scripture says, "He laid his hands on every one of them and healed them" (Luke 4:40). The healing stories of the New Testament encourage us to believe that health is possible. But the Bible does not support a naive view that promises a world free from pain. The crucifixion dispels such illusions.

Customarily, Jesus healed by "laying on of hands."[17] Following Jesus, the Church has used touch as one way to work toward a *healing oneing*, that is, for unity, wellness and *shalom*. Oil and the laying on of hands with prayers for the power of the Holy Spirit have been used to heal from the beginning of the Christian community.[18]

The Oil of Healing

The poet-author of Psalm 104 blessed God in a magnificent creation song that declares, "The earth is enriched by thy provision." Among the continuing creative acts of God listed in Psalm 104 are:

> bringing *bread* out of the earth
> and *wine* to gladden our hearts,
> *oil* to make our faces shine
> and bread to sustain our strength.

---

[15] Bruce C. Birch, "Biblical Faith and the Loss of Children," *The Christian Century*, October 26, 1983, p. 967.

[16] *Meditations of Julian of Norwich*, p. 44.

[17] For a good discussion of the role of touch in Jesus' ministry see Lindsey P. Pherigo, *The Great Physician, The Healing Stories in Luke and Their Meaning for Today* (New York: The Women's Division of Global Ministries of The United Methodist Church, 1983).

[18] For a helpful guide on the use of touch read Dolores Krieger, R.N., *The Therapeutic Touch, How to Use Your Hands to Help or Heal* (Englewood Cliffs, N.J.: Prentice-Hall, Inc. 1979).

Bread, wine and oil are those simple material blessings for which biblical writers often give thanks. We are all familiar with the line from the 23rd psalm, "Thou anointest my head with oil, my cup runneth over." These three blessings are so important that they become the liturgical elements in the public worship of Israel.

From earliest times, Israel offered prayers and anointed the sick with oil. Oil was used as a common medicine before the advent of modern medical practices. Leviticus 14 describes the use of oil in the ancient ritual of cleansing for a person who has been healed from skin diseases.

In Christian worship, bread and wine are the sacramental signs of the service of Holy Communion. Likewise, oil has been used from the beginning of Christianity as a sign of the power of God in anointing and healing. The writer of the book of James clearly indicates that the rite of anointing was used by the early Church for healing (James 5:13-16).

Oil was used in earliest Christianity as the Holy Spirit was invoked at the time of baptism and confirmation. Oil has continued to be administered as a seal which anoints the new believer as a member of the body of Christ. It is oil, blessed by a prayer, that has been used in healing rituals and in the last rites for the dying. Healing by laying on of hands with oil has a long and venerable tradition in Christianity. The practice is now being reconsidered for use in many Protestant churches.

Historically, a simple prayer was said over the oil asking God to bless it for healing. The pastor then dipped a thumb into the oil and made the sign of the cross on the sick person's forehead or hand with the oil. The ancient prayer was similar to this one: "We beseech the mercy of our Lord Jesus Christ, that all thy pain and sickness be put to flight and the blessing of health restored unto thee. Amen."

In the early Church, the laity, as well as the ordained, anointed the sick. The Episcopal church, a Protestant denomination that continues the practice of healing with oil, provides that a lay person may anoint using oil blessed by a bishop or priest. Some ministers in The United Methodist Church are also using oil with prayer as a sign of God's healing presence. I invite you, as you close this study together, to use the community signs of prayer and oil to invoke the power of God for the healing of suffering in the group. There is no need to disclose the nature of each person's suffering. All human beings suffer. If not for ourselves, we suffer for the pain that occurs in the lives of significant others—children, friends, spouses, and for the unknown and sometimes unnamed persons we see on television or read about in the newspapers.

Please sit in a circle for the worship so that everyone can participate in the liturgical action. A glass or pottery bowl may hold the oil.

Circle of Healing

Call To Prayer

Leader: Peace be to this place, and to all who gather here.
All: And peace also to you.
Leader: We come together in the name of Jesus Christ.
All: Yes! We assemble in the power of the whole people of God.

Hymn: "Stand by Me"   by Charles Albert Tindley[19]

("Stand by Me" can be done either as a corporate song or as a solo. If no piano is available, the hymn can be read as a prayer response.)

I.

Leader: When the storms of life are raging.
All: Stand by me.
Leader: When the storms of life are raging.
All: Stand by me.
Leader: When the world is tossing me, Like a ship upon the sea; Thou who rulest wind and water,
All: Stand by me.

---

[19] "Stand by Me," in *Songs of Zion* (Nashville: Abingdon, 1981), #41. Arrangement used by permission.

Stand by Me

Charles Albert Tindley, 1851-1933
Arr. by J. Jefferson Cleveland, 1937-
and Verolga Nix, 1933-

C. A. T. *Reverently - Moderate speed*

1. When the storms of life are rag - ing,
2. In the midst of trib - u - la - tion,
3. In the midst of faults and fail - ures, Stand by me;
4. In the midst of per - se - cu - tion,
5. When I'm grow - ing old and fee - ble,

When the storms of life are rag - ing, When the
In the midst of trib - u - la - tion, When the
In the midst of faults and fail - ures, Stand by me. When I
In the midst of per - se - cu - tion, When my
When I'm grow - ing old and fee - ble, When my

world is toss - ing me, Like a ship up - on the sea;
hosts of hell as - sail, And my strength be - gins to fail,
do the best I can, And my friends mis - un - der - stand,
foes in bat - tle ar - ray Un - der - take to stop my way,
life be - comes a bur - den, And I'm near - ing chil - ly Jor - dan,

Thou who rul - est wind and wa - ter,
Thou who nev - er lost a bat - tle,
Thou who know - est all a - bout me, Stand by me.
Thou who sav - ed Paul and Si - las,
O Thou "Lil - y of the Val - ley,"

123

II.

Leader: In the midst of tribulation,
All: Stand by me.
Leader: In the midst of tribulation,
All: Stand by me.
Leader: When the hosts of hell assail, And my strength begins to fail, Thou who never lost a battle,
All: Stand by me.

III.

Leader: In the midst of faults and failures,
All: Stand by me.
Leader: In the midst of faults and failures,
All: Stand by me.
Leader: When I do the best I can, And my friends misunderstand, Thou who knowest all about me,
All: Stand by me.

IV.

Leader: In the midst of persecution,
All: Stand by me.
Leader: In the midst of persecution,
All: Stand by me.
Leader: When my foes in battle array, Undertake to stop my way, Thou who saved Paul and Silas,
All: Stand by me.

V.

Leader: When I'm growing old and feeble,
All: Stand by me.
Leader: When I'm growing old and feeble,
All: Stand by me.
Leader: When my life becomes a burden, And I'm nearing chilly Jordan, O Thou "Lily of the Valley,"
All: Stand by me.

124

VI.

Leader: When the storms of life are raging,
All: Stand by me.
Leader: When the storms of life are raging,
All: Stand by me.
Leader: When the world is tossing me, Like a ship upon the sea; Thou who rulest wind and water,
All: Stand by me.

Bible Reading: Mark 6:7, 12-13 (They anointed with oil); James 5:13-15 (Is one of you ill?); 2 Corinthians 1:3-5 (God comforts us in trouble.)

Free Prayers for Those Who Are Suffering:

Blessing the Oil: *(Holding up a bowl of olive or other oil, the leader asks God's blessing with these or similar words:)*

Healing God, giver of life and health: bless this oil; so that, just as your apostles anointed those who suffered, may we who receive this oil gain comfort and peace. Send your Holy Spirit to us here that we may feel your healing power.

All: "So be it! Amen."

Anointing with Oil: *The leader will be seated and start the circle of healing. The leader will put a thumb in the oil and wait for a signal whether to put the oil on the forehead or hand of the person in the next seat.*

When the signal is given, the healer will make a sign of the cross on the head or hand while saying words of comfort. The words used by the healer will depend on the circumstances. They may be as simple as, "God bless and heal you," or perhaps, "May God give you the courage to face whatever suffering may come in your life." The person being signed will respond, "Amen," or, "thanks to be God."

The one who has received the sign will take the bowl of oil and repeat the process until all have received a blessing. The leader who began the anointing will be the last one to be signed and will then replace the bowl on the table.

Psalm 23: *(Psalm 23 may be prayed in the following words—or another translation may be used if so desired.)*

All: Lord, my shepherd, there's nothing I lack.
Leader: In fresh pastures you let me lie down;
You lead me beside quiet waters;
You restore me to life.

In order to show who you are,
You guide me in paths that are right.
Even walking through dark valleys,
I have no fear of harm.
For you yourself are with me;
Your rod and staff reassure me.

Right in front of my foes,
You lay out a feast for me.
You anoint my head with oil;
My cup is overflowing.

Goodness and love pursue me
Every day of my life;
God's house will be my home
As long as I may live.[20]

Closing Prayer

Leader: Our study is now over. We pray that the powerful and almighty God, who wraps, clasps and encloses us all around so as to never leave us; will grant us release from suffering, restoration of wholeness, and the gift of inner peace. In the name of Jesus, we pray.

All: We say, "Yes to Life! *Hallelujah Anyhow!* Amen."

---

[20] Gary Chamberlain, *The Psalms: A New Translation* (Nashville: The Upper Room, 1984). Used by permission. You might want to use a musical setting of Chamberlain's translation by Jane Marshall in *Psalms for Singing* (Nashville, The Upper Room, 1984), p. 28.

Discussion Questions

1. What do you think keeps the community of faith telling the old, old stories from the Bible—and newer ones too? What is the author's position on this question?

2. How do you understand the biblical word *shalom*? Can you give instances where the vision of *shalom* has seemed real in your life?

3. What does the author mean by the phrase "remembering into the future"? Have you discovered special ways of remembering the past in order to create a more open future? Share some of the ways you remember into the future.

4. How did you feel about the liturgy of healing? Have you ever used oil before in a service of worship? Do you think it would be beneficial for the life of your congregation?

Spiritual Exercises

If the group would like to explore other avenues of spiritual healing these two books are worth exploring: Hallie Iglehart, "Women as the New Healers" in *Womanspirit* (San Francisco: Harper & Row, Publishers, 1983) and Delores Krieger, *The Therapeutic Touch, How to Use Your Hands to Help or to Heal* (Englewood Cliffs, N.J.: Prentice-Hall, Inc., 1979). For rituals especially for women write to WATER *(The Women's Alliance for Theology, Ethics and Ritual)* at 8035 13th Street, Suites 1 & 3, Silver Spring, Maryland 20910.

Further Reading

Clark, Linda, Marion Ronan, Eleanor Walker. *Image-Breaking, Image-Building, a Handbook for Creative Worship with Women of Christian Tradition*. New York: The Pilgrim Press, 1981.

Griggs, Donald L. *Translating the Good News through Teaching Activities*. Nashville: Abingdon, 1980.

Iglehart, Hallie. *Womanspirit, a Guide to Women's Wisdom*. San Francisco: Harper & Row, 1983.

Jones, Nathan. *Sharing the Old, Old Story, Educational Ministry in the Black Community*. Winona, Minnesota: Saint Mary's Press, 1982. Other materials are available from Ethnic Communications Outlet, 5342 South University Avenue, Chicago, Illinois 60615.

Kollar, Nathan. *Songs of Suffering*. Minneapolis: Winston Press, 1982.

Krieger, Dolores. *The Therapeutic Touch, How to Use Your Hands to Help or to Heal*. Englewood Cliffs, N.J.: Prentice-Hall, Inc., 1979. Particularly see chapter 9 "The Symbolic Experience."

Pherigo, Lindsey P. *The Great Physician, The Healing Stories in Luke and Their Meaning for Today*. New York: The Women's Division of Global Ministries of The United Methodist Church, 1983.*

Simonton, O. Carl, Stephanie Matthew-Simonton, James L. Creighton. *Getting Well Again*. New York: Bantam Books, 1978.

Stomberg, Jean, ed. *Sharing One Bread, Sharing One Mission, The Eucharist as Missionary Event*. Geneva: World Council of Churches Mission Series, 1983.

Westerhoff, John H. III. *Living the Faith Community, the Church that Makes a Difference*. Minneapolis; Winston Press, 1985.

---

*Available from the Service Center, General Board of Global Ministries, 7820 Reading Road, Cincinnati, Ohio 45237.

Planning the Study

Introduction

A study on Suffering and the Christian Community of Faith is always timely. Suffering comes to us through many relationships and contexts—individual, familial, communal, national, and global. What affects one of us affects all of us. Suffering comes to us in many kinds of experience—mental, emotional, physical, and spiritual. It is a common thread binding all humankind.

Our study text is written by one who has known the tragedy and despair of suffering and has struggled and agonized over the meaning of suffering in the context of her faith. Her personal experiences of suffering have led her to a deep level of empathy with the sufferings of others around the world. She deals with personal and relational tragedy and loss, with personal suffering and transformation in the Spirit, with the larger suffering experienced through the evils of oppression, hunger, and powerlessness. These are experiences for you and me to know and to try to understand better within the Christian community of faith.

In this study, we will acquaint ourselves anew with the Suffering God we see in the Bible, especially the Suffering Son, Jesus the Christ. It is essential for us to let the power and grace of this Suffering God, the strength and grace of the Suffering Son, and the comfort and grace of the Suffering Spirit break in upon our lives if we are to be sustained in our faith, grow in our understanding, and have hope for our future. God becomes one with us and with all others who suffer, giving us the grace to endure and to overcome.

129

Using the Text and the Teacher's Guide

There are a variety of ways this study may be carried out by the leader and the group. The basic study book for this spiritual growth study is *Hallelujah Anyhow! Suffering and the Christian Community of Faith*, written by Diedra Kriewald. It includes discussion questions and spiritual exercises. This teacher's guide includes additional questions and exercises and suggests prayers, hymns, and readings which go with the study book. You will not be able to do everything suggested. Choose what is best for your group. Try to include a balance of spiritual exercises and discussion questions.

Preparation by the Leader

Read carefully the basic text. You may also read and reflect upon some passages of Scripture you have found helpful in understanding suffering. As you read, recall some significant, life-changing, "watershed" experiences of suffering within the Christian community that you have experienced or know about. These reflections and experiences could be noted in a "Journal on Suffering and the Christian Community," which you may want to keep, beginning with your first reading of the text and your initial preparation for the course. You also will find current resources almost daily in the newspaper and in magazines and religious journals. Clipping and keeping and using stories of others' struggles with suffering will add depth and breadth to your study.

In addition to the text, the Bible, and current periodicals, there are other books you will want to read and/or be familiar with. Diedra Kriewald suggests a number at the end of each chapter. Leslie Weatherhead's *The Will of God* is an excellent resource for helping us understand the place of God and God's will in our suffering. Paul Tournier's *Creative Suffering* helps us begin to see creative uses we can make of suffering. John Claypool's *Tracks of a Fellow Struggler* is helpful for those who face personal and terminal illness in their family. Rabbi Harold Kushner's *When Bad*

*Things Happen to Good People** provides another personal world about individual and family suffering, and gives some good words on the role of God in suffering, as seen from the Jewish faith-stance. Paul Schilling's *God and Human Anguish* is a careful and helpful writing, from the biblical and theological view, with emphasis on the suffering of God in the suffering of humanity.

There are other resources that will be helpful in planning worship time as part of the class time. The *Supplement to the Book of Hymns,*+ *Songs of Zion,*+ *Everflowing Streams*, and *Sisters and Brothers Sing!** are useful books of music and hymns.+ Other books to help with worship include *The Worship Handbook*, Langford and Jones; *Wholeness in Worship,** Sharon and Thomas Neufer Emswiler; *Notes on Love and Courage* and *There Is a Place Where You Are Not Alone*, both by Hugh Prather; *Creative Brooding* and *Lord, Could You Make It a Little Better*, both by Robert Raines; *Prayers*, Michel Quoist; *Everyday Prayers*, William Barclay; *A Guide to Prayer for Ministers and Other Servants* edited by Rueben Job. There are pertinent chapters in both of my books, *A Sprig of Hope* and *Holy Moments*+; *The Healing Fountain,** edited by Betty Thompson; and *Heads Bowed Together*, edited by Ann Simon.

Two books that will be useful in other ways are Beth E. Rhude's *Live the Questions Now,** an insightful writing to help in developing the prayer and spiritual life and on how to keep a journal; and Joanna Roger Macy's *Despair and Personal Power in the Nuclear Age,** very good for suggestions on group experiences of visioning and imaging. These will be good for the leader, for members of the class, and for resources in the classroom.

Overview

Plan for six sessions, using the author's six chapters as a basic format. Each session or chapter could be compressed

---

* Available from the Service Center. Check current *Catalog* for ordering information.

+ Available from Cokesbury, 201 Eighth Avenue, South, P.O. Box 801, Nashville, TN 37202.

to a one-hour consideration or expanded to a minimum of six two-hour sessions. Following are brief summaries of these chapters and general questions to consider.

Chapter 1 focuses on the tragedy the author experienced at San Jose Iturbi, Mexico in the summer of 1962. Consider questions about the place of sin or evil in suffering, the role of God in suffering, and how the author struggled to cope with this nightmarish experience.

Chapter 2 deals with Teresa of Avila, her suffering and self-inflicted illnesses, her dramatic conversion, and her new-found life and faith. What part does mind play in body sickness/health? How does one find the kind of relationship with Christ that changed and sustained Teresa?

Chapter 3 deals with a worldwide and local experience of suffering—oppression. Consider the effect of oppression on the oppressor and the oppressed and look at some close-to-home kinds of oppression we all know. Where is God in times of oppression?

Chapter 4 deals with the crisis of world hunger. The author looks at physical and spiritual famine. What does it mean to live in a world where both physical and spiritual famine can be relieved and know we are doing little to move toward significant or lasting relief? Consider some of the personal and national priority questions/issues we encounter when we look honestly at ourselves and those starving around us.

Chapter 5 confronts the suffering experienced in powerlessness. The struggle for power in this country, in Central America, in South Africa, and in other parts of the world only dramatizes what millions of human beings feel every day. How do we go about "setting the captives [the powerless] free"?

Chapter 6 is on our journey toward wholeness, the pilgrimage possible for all of us. What are some signs and symbols necessary for this journey? How do we sustain each other on our journeys? Here is where we find purpose and meaning in the experience of the Christian community of faith.

Study Session I

Assignments

Reading: Read the preface and chapter 1 of the text.
Wall Displays: Display some pictures/paintings depicting both human suffering and ways suffering is or may be relieved. Quote some appropriate and helpful passages of Scripture on posters or newsprint such as Deuteronomy 33:27a; Romans 8:18; Psalm 121:7-8; and other passages that show God's grace and support in times of suffering. Also, some quotes from writings that have a word of strength and help, such as Viktor Frankl's "He [or she] who has a why to live for can survive almost any how."

Worship Resources

Hymns: "O God Our Help in Ages Past," p. 28 (change "its sons" to people in stanza 5), "Standing on the Promises," p. 121, "Guide Me, O Thou Great Jehovah," p. 271, *The Book of Hymns;* "Leaning on the Everlasting Arms," p. 53, "Jesus, Savior, Pilot Me," p. 49, *Songs of Zion*
Prayer: You may want to pray as a class the prayer in hymn #125, "Jesus, Lover of My Soul," *The Book of Hymns.*

Purpose

To see how the "stories" of our lives reveal the agony of suffering and the goodness of knowing God's grace in the midst of our suffering, through our own inner struggle with God and through the grace of God in others.

Group Experience

1. This opening session can best begin by talking about "canonical" stories and our stories and the importance of knowing and claiming our stories as important and authentic. Then, the leader may read excerpts from "San

Jose Iturbi." The introductory paragraph and the poem could be read, and the group can reflect upon their feelings about this story.

2. The author writes, "Most mourners find some negative ways of handling tragedy." What are some "negative ways" you have seen others handle tragedy? What are some "positive ways" we might keep in mind for ourselves and suggest to others?

3. Ask the group to reflect on their "theology of tragedy" or "theology of suffering." What you want is for them to reflect and understand their views or beliefs about tragedy/suffering and God. Ask them to spend 5-6 minutes reflecting and then writing this "theology." Then, invite them to share with one another, one-on-one, some of their reflections. In what ways has the church provided, or not provided, those in the group a "working theology with which to handle tragedy"?

4. The author's third paragraph after her first poem is full of material for questions/discussion. Read it aloud and then discuss: Does God cause or predestine tragedy and suffering? What is the basis for your beliefs about this? Is suffering caused by "devils"? By "sin"? How would you respond to the suggestion that these deaths were "a part of God's larger plan" or that this accident (or similar suffering) is God's will"? Invite the group to discuss the relationship of some of the following to suffering: luck, chance, fate, our choices, God's will, our genes, human error, mistakes, sin, evil.

5. The author talks of how the Irenaean school of thinking about suffering in the Christian community has helped her. This view says, ". . . The world is [still] under construction." Ask the group to discuss if this view is helpful in coping with suffering. Are we to find comfort from knowing that the world is still being created? If so, how does this view help us deal with suffering?

6. Discuss three statements in the text: "Some deaths do have dignity and purpose"; "Some deaths are essentially meaningless"; "All suffering does not have a noble end." Let the group share with one another some deaths that have had dignity or purpose. Describe some deaths you have known that have *seemed* to be meaningless. Does suffering ever/often/always/never have a noble end? Talk over some of Tournier's writings in *Creative Suffering*.

The chapter, "Bad Things," in my book, *Holy Moments*, suggests that, for some experiences in life, "there may be no answers." Ask the group to share how it feels about this suggestion.

7. The text talks of "existential dread" as the loss of present meaning and the fear of the future. Are there ways we can prepare ourselves for suffering so that we do not experience this? Let the group share one-on-one some of these ways. Then, ask each to respond and list on newsprint her or his suggestions. The author says she had to "learn to trust the universe all over again." Once our trust (in God, others, or self) is broken, what are some ways of having it restored?

8. Ask each member of the group to sit quietly and to reflect for two minutes when you pose the question: If some tragic experience came to one of your loved ones or to you, how would you feel if someone said to you, "Hang on to Jesus." What are some "handles" by which we might "hang on to Jesus"—symbols? words? scripture? stories? hymns? music? images? art pieces?

9. The author's exercise on symbolic garments we wear to cover ourselves in time of suffering could be most helpful. Discuss not only "what we do wear" but also what might "be more helpful for us to wear."

10. An appropriate closing could be to ask the group to sit quietly and meditate for a few moments. Close by reading or praying the words of the hymn, "Stand by Me," p. 123 of this book.

Preparation for Session II

Read chapter 2 of the text. Have someone share a summary of Leslie Weatherhead's *The Will of God*. Another can tell the class some highlights of the life of Teresa of Avila. Prepare some quotes on newsprint from Scripture or other writings depicting the personal journey from suffering toward wholeness (Jesus in the wilderness, in Gethsemane, on the cross).

Study Session II

Assignments

Reading: Read chapter 2 in the text and some background material on individual sickness, suffering, and grace from books suggested in the text and the guide.

Art and Room Displays: An art piece of the *Pieta* or a painting or facsimile of the sculpture would be good to have in the room. Ask the class members to image the scene of Teresa in front of the statue of the wounded Christ, wiping Jesus' wounds with her tears as Teresa saw herself doing as Martha, and then have them express their feelings in art—painting, drawing, word, symbol, clay molding, poem, song, or other. Display these in the class.

Worship Resources

Hymns: "Balm in Gilead," p. 123, "Sometimes I Feel Like a Motherless Chile," p. 83, "His Eye Is on the Sparrow," p. 33, *Songs of Zion;* "Just As I Am," p. 119, "Jesus, My Strength, My Hope, p. 253, "Have Thine Own Way, Lord," p. 154, "I Am Thine, O Lord," p. 159, "Jesus, Thy Boundless Love to Me," p. 259, *The Book of Hymns;* and "Because He Lives," p. 864, *Supplement to the Book of Hymns*
Prayers: Luke 22:39-44, Luke 4:1-14a; The prayer by Peter Marshall on p. 259 of *A Guide to Prayer for Ministers and Other Servants* edited by Rueben Job; "Free Flight," p. 48, "Psalm of a Modern Woman," p. 34, and "Bedrock," p. 33 of *Images: Women in Transition**

Purpose

This session is to acquaint us with the sickness, suffering, struggles, and strength of Teresa of Avila and to let her

---

* Available from the Service Center. Check current catalog for ordering information.

story become our story and our story be one with her story so that the healing, renewing, and sustaining grace of Christ can touch and empower us.

Group Experience

This section gives us the opportunity to look at our own individual sicknesses and handicaps and to find ways both to endure and overcome.

1. Mark 10:46-52 is the story of Bartimaeus, whose blindness was healed by Jesus. Jesus asks him, "What do you want me to do for you?" Ask the group to consider some questions raised by our text and by this story in Mark: Do we (as the church or as individuals) assume that we *know* what people need in order to be cured? Do we give people an opportunity to tell us what they want/need from us? How can we structure opportunities for this kind of feedback?

2. Read aloud the rabbinic tale quoted from Elie Wiesel. Discuss: What is the place of ritual in our journey through life? How important is it to know how to "light the fire," "say the prayer," "know the place," and "tell the story"? Ask the group to share experiences where this kind of ritual has been healing (such as holy communion, baptism, or anointing with oil). Is it "enough" just to "know the story"? What is it about retelling/reliving a "story" that is healing/sustaining?

3. The author says we are guilty of "spiritual amnesia" and have forgotten the influential place of women in our Judeo-Christian tradition. Invite each member of the group to engage in the following exercise: Sit quietly for 3-5 minutes; recall some story of a woman of faith (from the Bible or church history or from your own personal experiences); write down a few sentences about that woman's life and what made her influential; then write some of the ways this woman's story has influenced you and share her story with someone else or the larger group.

4. The quote of Teresa on page 26 which begins "When I left. . ." describes an experience common to many children and youth today. The "separation" that countless numbers of children and youth feel from their mother and/or father is a contemporary type of "suffering" worth discussing. What are some ways the church can be helpful to parents and children who go through this suffering? Ask each member of the group to think about painful separation(s) they have known, reflect on those, and then share with the group some of the things that helped during that time.

5. From the text, look at some of the "critical others" in Teresa's life—her mother who died when she was 12, her father, the "friendly nun" at the Augustinian boarding school, and her "pious widowed uncle." How did the "good" these persons were doing for her and the "truth" they were imposing on her bring about her "suffering"? Note the dramatic shift from a healthy young woman to a very sickly young woman after she was at the boarding school. Talk about some of the "good" things we do to others that may not be good for them, some "truths" we give others that may not be true for them. Are there ways today through which the church and we, as individual Christians, cause this kind of suffering for others? How can we help others to experience their own good and come to their own truths?

6. Read the text describing Teresa's life from the time she became a religious until she was 39. Can we force ourselves to be religious, to live a spiritually disciplined life? If so, what are some of the benefits? Some of the dangers? Are there times we should force ourselves to persevere even though we experience pain and sickness? When/What are some of those times?

7. Invite the group to do some imaging. Re-tell the story of Teresa's experience in the chapel before the statue of Christ. Ask the members of the group to close their eyes and sit quietly and try to image the wounded Christ in the arms of Mary. Live into this moment in any way possible. Look into the face of Jesus; see his wounds and his bleeding and suffering; touch him and comfort him in his pain; try to feel yourself wiping the wounds of Jesus. Give ample time for this to be experienced as fully as possible by each one in the group. Ask each one to reflect and write some lines on the meaning of Jesus' suffering, on what his suffering means to

us in our suffering, on how we can benefit from his suffering, on how we can relieve some of his suffering, on what it means to hear the suffering Jesus say, "Peace I give to you. . . ."

8. Augustine's life was a saving paradigm for Teresa. He confessed himself a sinner, and this helped her. How are we helped in our weakness/sin/suffering by knowing of another's weakness/sin/suffering? Who do we want with us when we struggle/suffer/sin—one who is right, righteous, and whole or one who knows he/she is broken and will be with us in our brokenness? Why? Is this why/how the suffering of Jesus can be and is healing and restoring for us in our suffering? Let the group talk about how Jesus' suffering is healing for them.

9. Compare the life of Teresa before and after her conversion experience before the statue of Jesus: her prayer life; her view of herself, her suffering, her illnesses; her works; her belief that the life of prayer and the life of action go together.

10. Look at the journey Teresa made: A "limping self-image"; "internal self-talk that was positive"; confident attitudes about herself; "courage to try a new method of communicating with God." These steps seem healthy and productive, when viewed from an overall perspective. Ask the group, "Where do you see yourself on this spectrum or journey?" How do we keep open to ourselves, to others, to God so that we can keep moving toward wholeness and "perfection" (to use Wesley's term)?

11. Invite the group to talk about the place of prayer in healing. Are prayers for healing always heard and answered by God? How? How does prayer for the healing of others affect their healing? Why are prayers of the community important in times of suffering/healing?

12. Ask the group to respond and discuss the meaning of the author's concluding statements, namely, that God calls each of us to take charge of our suffering, to look for help in the community of faith, and to work for the welfare of our neighbor. How can we know if God calls each of us to do this? How do we prepare ourselves to respond appropriately?

Preparation for Session III

Read Part II, Chapter I of the text. Alan Paton's *Instrument of Thy Peace* and Bishop Tutu's *Hope and Suffering* have some very pertinent chapters in them. A reading and sharing of these concerns could help set the stage for a timely session on South Africa and oppression. The story of the oppression and march to freedom of Israelites in Exodus and the first six chapters of Daniel provide helpful scriptural settings for oppression.

Study Session III

Assignments

Reading: Read Part II, Chapter 1 of the text. Read some of the story of the Israelites in Egypt and the journey toward Canaan in Exodus and the first six chapters of Daniel, which describe some of the experiences of the children of Israel in Babylon. Read Isaiah 58:6 and 61:1-2 and Luke 4:16-21 to get some sense of the calling to minister to the oppressed.

Art Work and Displays: Display some pictures that depict the plight of oppressed peoples. Pictures from national church and secular magazines show the suffering of oppressed peoples in Iran, Afghanistan, Poland, South Africa, Ethiopia, and other countries. Invite class members to bring and post art or pictures or news stories about oppression.

Worship Resources

Hymns: "Make Me Captive, Lord," p. 184, "Take up Thy Cross," p. 160, and "Hope of the World," p. 161, of *The Book of Hymns;* "We'll Understand It Better By and By," p. 55, "I've Been 'Buked," p. 143, "Precious Lord, Take My Hand," p. 179, "We've Come This Far By Faith," p. 192, *Songs of Zion Prayers and Other Writings:* "Prayer for Justice," p. 62, "The Mid-time," p. 30, and "A Call to Worship and Prayer,"

p. 124, *Images, Women in Transition;* Prayer, "It is Dark," p. 138-140 of *Prayers* by Quoist. "I Hold the Bandages. . . ," pp. 20-21 in *Creative Brooding* by Robert Raines; excerpts from *Unyoung, Uncolored, Unpoor,* Colin Morris. Use the hymn, "A Mighty Fortress Is Our God," by Martin Luther, as a corporate prayer for the group. (See p. 57 of *Everflowing Streams.*) On pp. 200-201 in *Prayers for Ministers and Other Servants* edited by Rueben Job, the lines by Henri Nouwen speak eloquently of the "leadership" needed in our day.

"An old rabbi was once asked why so few people were finding God. He wisely replied that people are not willing to look that low. Jesus was born in a stable, and God is especially concerned for the poorest, the lowliest, the lost, and the neglected" (from *Liberation of Life* by Harvey and Lois Seifert).

Purpose

To become aware in new ways of "the devouring fire" of oppression that is in our midst in this country and in other countries around the world and to gain some new insights into how we may help to "set at liberty those who are oppressed."

Group Experience

1. It will be important to have some common understandings within the group of some of the words which will be used frequently in this session. Read again the description of the words "oppression," "oppressors," and the "oppressed." Then, talk about these definitions and put a "working definition" on newsprint. There may be some in the group who will have experienced oppression first-hand; if they are ready at the start of the class, let them share their experiences.
2. We usually think of oppression as a phenomenon which happens in other countries. Focus some time on oppression in the U.S. Here, some very personal stories of exploitation and dehumanization may pour forth; women, Blacks, and other ethnic minority persons have been victimized at all levels of our society and in parts of the country. What are some ways the church and members of the class can begin to "set at liberty those who are oppressed"? Let the class

work in groups of 4-6 to try to be very specific about groups being oppressed and come up with 3-5 ways to give support to and find relief for the oppressed. Share these with the total group and put on newsprint.

3. Take a newspaper and go through it, marking, cutting, and posting on the walls the stories in that day's paper about oppression. Read and share some of those stories with the group. Which of these have to do with religious oppression? Political? Racial? Sexual? Is the church involved in any of these, siding with either the oppressor or the oppressed? How is this so? Discuss how the church can become/is involved in the alleviation of oppression in some nations (e.g., Ethiopia or South Africa).

4. Two feelings many have when they see so much oppression in the world are guilt and helplessness. Ask the class to gather one-on-one and discuss whether are not they feel any guilt about the plight of the oppressed. (Note: Some persons may not. Be careful not to impose on everyone a feeling everyone may not share.) Then, have some of these feelings shared with the group. What are some ways the group can help deal with this guilt? Again, in one-on-one communication, talk about feelings of helplessness. Share these with the group. Discuss: Are we helpless? Are there things we can do? What are they? How can the church as a community give us a sense of belonging and helping?

5. Turn to pp. 47-48 to read again the exercise the author calls "clustering." Follow steps 1-4 as an individual and group exercise to help focus on suffering caused by oppression.

6. The text tells powerful "stories of courage" of Christians who have become martyrs because of their faith in Christ and their standing with/and for the oppressed. Of Archbishop Romero, the author writes, "He followed Jesus too well . . . took too many stands, upset too many tables and preached too many dangerous sermons on the subject of political and economic reform." What are some of the risks the church and we, as individuals, take if we "follow Jesus too well"? Where do we find the courage, the strength, the will to do this? Let the members of the class tell of persons they have known who have shown courage in standing for the oppressed.

142

7. Talk about the work and witness of the mothers in Argentina. Ask the class to try to project themselves into the lives of these mothers and feel what they must have felt. What did they do? What was the effect of their witness? How was the church involved? What would you do, or try to do, if your teenage son/daughter was missing?

8. Adolfo Esquivel dreamed he saw Christ on the cross wearing an Indian poncho, the dress of the poor. Mother Teresa has said, "Jesus comes among us today disguised as the poor." Do you agree with this statement? If this is true, what does this mean for the mission and ministry of the church and for each of us in it?

9. The story of Fannie Lou Hamer tells of courage in the face of racial oppression toward Blacks and other ethnic minorities in this country today. What are some ways, if there are any, in which this oppression has loosened in recent years? What is The United Methodist Church's position regarding oppression and the rights of all people? (Refer to the *Discipline* and the "Social Creed.")

10. The author tells us "that God is present and active wherever there is suffering caused by oppression." What is God "doing" while oppression persists? How are we called upon—and to do what—in order to reveal the love and justice of God? Is God waiting to be present and active in and through us? If so, how? This could lead to some very honest and painful confession and to some real commitment to act and speak with and on behalf of the oppressed.

11. A good way to end this session would be to have each person write a new covenant with herself/himself to begin in specific ways to speak and to act to help "set at liberty those who are oppressed."

Preparation for Session IV

Read Part II, Chapter 4 on "Famine." Read Matthew 5:3-14, with attention given to 5:6. Read pages 6-22 of *Beyond Brokenness* (Smith & Barndt) to get a capsule view of brokenness and wholeness in our world. Be prepared with some up-to-date statistics on hunger in various parts of the world.

Study Session IV

Assignments

Reading: Read Part II, chapter 4 of the text. Look in a good concordance and read several passages of Scripture having to do with famine and hunger.

Art and Room Displays: Prepare two meals for the center of attention—one like we might eat at a lavish banquet in this country and one like the starving in Ethiopia might have. Divide the class into six groups and label them the six continents; take 50 raisins and apportion them to each group according to the percentage of food used by each continent; let the class see dramatized the disproportionate amount used by the western world and the U.S. in particular. Have some pictures of those suffering from famine. There are powerful quotes for posters in Colin Morris's *Include Me Out* such as: "But then, we can explain away anything we do, except possibly, why it is that our mountain of words brings forth only a gnat of humane action" (p. 19). "Your theology, fancy or plain, is what you are when the talking stops and the action starts" (p. 30). "We are a rich Church in a hungry world. That is why our message rings hollow and our influence declines" (p. 67).

Worship Resources

Hymns: "Re-Member Me," p. 86, "I Am Meat and I Am Drink," p. 83, *Sisters and Brothers Sing!;* "Break Thou the Bread of Life," p. 369, "The Lord's My Shepherd," p. 68, "Let Us Break Bread Together," p. 330, "For the Beauty of the Earth," p. 35, "All Things Bright and Beautiful," p. 34, *The Book of Hymns;* "His Eye Is on the Sparrow," p. 33, "Over My Head," p. 167, *Songs of Zion*

Prayers and Other Readings: Amos 8:4-7. "Did You Ever Cry, Jesus?," p. 93, "Feed My Lambs," p. 106, in *Images: Women in Transition;* prayer on 313, pp. 245-246, in *Prayers for Ministers and Other Servants*

Purpose

To get an understanding of the widespread suffering and starvation caused by famine and see how we can bring relief to those who suffer from physical and spiritual hunger.

Group Experience

1. At the beginning of the chapters, the author quotes Amos 8:11, which says God "will send famine on the land." Do we take this as literally true? If so, what does it mean? Is God responsible for sending famine? How do the class members feel about God "sending" famine?

2. Talk about various meanings and uses of the word "hunger." What are some ways we hunger that are positive and helpful? Negative and hurtful? What are some of the characteristics of one who is physically hungry? Spiritually hungry? What are the results of hungering spiritually, physically? Let the group talk about ways we can help allevate spiritual hunger, physical hunger. Put comments on newsprint.

3. Look at some of the biblical stories involving famine. What is God's role in bringing famine? What is the role of various people—religious leaders, political leaders, people in general—in causing famine to occur?

4. What are some of the primary and secondary causes of hunger in the world today (Primary—greed, misuse of power, fear, etc.; secondary—political policies, poor distribution systems, illiteracy, etc.) List these for all to see and reflect upon. Divide the class with groups of 4-5; have one-half the class discuss the primary causes and how we can work to overcome them and one-half discuss the secondary causes and how we can work to overcome them. Put on newsprint in classroom.

5. Look at the statistics (p. 71) for death from famine. Ask the group to think of ways we can "humanize" and "individualize" these statistics so that we become aware of the magnitude of the problem. Again, the sense of helplessness comes to us: "The problem is great. I am only one. What can I do?" What are some things anyone of us can do? List them. Pray. Write the President. Write members of Congress. Write the Secretary of State and the Secretary of Agriculture, etc.

6. Read Revelation 6:1-17 and the author's words on this passage. There are lessons to be learned from this vision: sin (setting out to conquer) *has inevitable consequences* in war, famine, death. There is a cyclical effect to these four horse riders—conquering leads to war to famine to death and back to conquering again. How does this show, as one writer puts it, "the futility of evil"? Reflect upon how famine is the side effect of power struggles and wars. Are there any ways we can ever hope to get that message across to the leaders of all the nations?

7. The text reads, "clearly peace and justice issues belong together." How is this so? What are some ways famine results from our "making for war" and not for peace"? Ask someone to research and be prepared to share with the class how much could be done to alleviate hunger and hunger-related problems if we used some of our "defense" money to feed the hungry. Is this author correct in saying that "famine will [not] be eliminated unless and until wars cease"? Talk about what it would mean to "Beat our swords into plowshares." How can we make this vision a reality?

8. One of the justifications some persons use is to say, "Let the poor fend for themselves" or "If they would only try, they could make it," or "We've always had them (the poor and starving) and we always will" is Jesus' statement in Matthew 26:11. Let the class read that in its original context in Deuteronomy 15:11 and 15:4-5. In groups of 4-5, let the class talk about what this passage means, namely since "we have the poor with us always," do we just accept this and do nothing? What can we do?

9. Colin Morris, in talking about the church getting its priorities in order, says, "Christianity is simply doing costly things for the sake of Christ." What are some "costly things" each of us *may* do for the sake of the hungry? Which of those are we willing to do? Let each one covenant with herself/himself to do one or more of these as soon as possible.

10. The author talks about Yahweh weeping bitterly over Israel and singing a lament for the suffering ones. For those who starve, of what good is it to know that God weeps and

146

laments? Is that word comforting to us, only because we are not starving? What that is helpful *does* God say to or do with those who are starving?

11. Ask the class to read the poem, "From Jaini B.—with Love" and talk about ways God can "come to" a starving person in India or Africa or anywhere.

12. The text reads, "Guilt will not motivate us to feed the poor." Are there times when guilt has been a/the motivating factor? Let the class discuss instances of which they may be aware. Does it matter *what* motivates a person or nation to feed the hungry, as long as they are fed? The text continues, "Choosing freely to follow a compassionate God is the right reason" for feeding the hungry. This may be the "best" reason, but is there just *one* "right" reason? Ask the class to share as many varied reasons as they can think of (give 3-5 minutes to do this). You may then want to prioritize these.

Preparation for Session V

Read Part II, chapter 5 of the text. Read the temptation story of Jesus, Luke 4:1-14a. Have someone read selected portions from one of the following (or other good writings on the struggles of the powerless) and share a brief synopsis with the class: *Room to Be People*, Bonino; *The Cry of My People*, Esther and Mortimer Arias. Read Daniel, chapters 1-6.

Study Session V

Assignments

Reading: Read Part II, Chapter 5 in the text. Read some background material on powerlessness (general and group) of your own choosing or some from M. Scott Peck's *People of the Lie* (esp. chapters 3, 4, 7); T. I. Rubin's *Reconciliations;* Martin Luther King's *Where Do We Go from Here?;* or selected chapters from S. Paul Schilling's *God and Human Anguish.*
Art and Room Display: Find some vivid pictures of individual

and group powerlessness in recent issues of *Time, Life,* or *Newsweek,* and post these on walls. Get quotes from Quoist's *Prayers* or Taines' *Creative Brooding* or Colin Morris's *Include Me Out* and put on newsprint, to express feeling of powerlessness that individuals and groups have. Post a blank piece of newsprint, headed "Experiences of Powerlessness," and ask the group to write on it words or phrases to depict powerlessness they know.

Hymns: "Nobody Knows the Trouble I See," p. 170, "Precious Lord, Take My Hand," p. 179, "Kum Ba Yah," p. 139, *Songs of Zion;* "My Hope is Built," p. 222, "Trust and Obey," p. 223, "Eternal God, Whose Power Upholds," p. 476, *The Book of Hymns;* "Lonesome Valley," p. 120, "Peace Like River," p. 51, *Sisters and Brothers Sing! Prayers and Other Readings:* Psalm 121, Psalm 139, Isaiah 42:1-4, Matthew 8:23-27, Luke 1:46-55, "The Journey," p. 135, "The Future Breaking In," p. 142, "Free Flight," p. 48, "For Every Woman," p. 52, "The Image of God," p. 73 in *Images: Women in Transition.* Read "Free At Last," p. 80, "Love Lifted Me," p. 71 in *Songs of Zion.* Read chapters 4-8 of Joanna Rogers Macy's *Despair and Personal Power in the Nuclear Age* for helpful insight and for rich experiences to be done by the group.

Purpose

In this chapter the author confronts us with some illnesses and infirmities that maim us and take away our control of life. We want to become aware of our finiteness and humanness and try to learn some ways of helping others cope, or to learn ways to cope ourselves, when we are faced with situations in which one's power is lost or curtailed.

Group Experience

One way to begin this session would be to have someone be prepared to share a story of someone who has lived a healthy, active, productive life and then has come face to face with a serious illness. This could be one's own story or the story of another. This will "bring to life" the reality of powerlessness as described by the first part of this chapter.

1. Alzheimer's Disease, cancer, porphyria, and AIDS are four illnesses touched on in the text. The writer tells us, "human beings are still powerless against the onslaught of destructive disease." Are we *always* powerless? *Completely* powerless? Are there not *some* things we can do when faced with this kind of illness? (Read Norman Cousins' books, *The Anatomy of An Illness* and *The Healing Heart,* to see what he suggests we can do.)

2. What happens to the human spirit when confronted by a permanently crippling or life-ending illness? Talk about how different persons react to this reality. What are some of our options? What part does the sick one play? Do others play? How can the church help? Where and how does God come in? How can we get persons to relate meaningfully to God during this time? (Granger Westburg's *Good Grief* would be helpful to use here.)

3. Ask the group to read Scott Peck's definition of evil on p. 90. Is the definition, "Evil is 'live' spelled backwards," helpful? Ask the class to take a sheet of paper and reflect for 2-3 minutes on how they would define evil. Then, write out a personal definition of evil. One-on-one communication followed by sharing with the total group could well lead the group to a definition of evil.

4. If evil, as Peck says, "is that which opposes the life force," what are some of those things which oppose the life force today?

5. The tornadoes which killed many persons in 1985 in Ohio and Pennsylvania were "not God's work. . . ," said a survivor. To what or whom do you attribute storms and natural disasters, before which we are powerless, as they wreak havoc and cause suffering and death? Is the phrase used by insurance companies, "acts of God," an appropriate way to describe these? Why? Why not? How do you "fit God" into a plan for this earth that includes natural storms and violence?

6. We also suffer from powerlessness when individuals overwhelm us or overpower us—crimes of rape, murder, kidnap, robbery, etc. The incidence of this kind of suffering is high in this country. What are some positive ways the church can become involved in our society to help relieve

this kind of suffering and violence? What are some things we as individuals can do? As local churches?

7. We usually think of certain groups of persons as suffering from powerlessness—Blacks, the poor, women, children, Native Americans, migrant workers. . . . Who are others that the class would list as powerless? Ask the class to reflect for a few minutes on the *kinds* of suffering powerlessness brings.

8. The author tells us, "The Christian community gives the assurance . . . that suffering can be redeemed." Is this true in all cases? Why? Why not? How is suffering "redeemed"? How do we keep the words "suffering can be redeemed" from being trite? empty? superficial? condescending? meaningless? wishful thinking?

9. Let the class divide into groups of 3-4. Ask them to recall the stories of courage of Elizabeth Cook and Ludwig Van Beethoven. Then, ask them to share with the others a story of courage of someone they have known. What part(s) of the person in the story experienced powerlessness? How did this affect that person? How did that person demonstrate her/his courage? Where do you think she/he got the strength, grace, courage? What affect has that person's life and courage had on others?

10. The text suggests a three-stage paradigm for dealing with suffering: "Name the Pain", "Enter into the Suffering, and Let It Go"; and "Witness to the Power." Think of examples of personal or group suffering where this has been a helpful and productive pattern. Talk about how God's power and presence move through people and experiences such as this. How does God work in individuals, in leaders and followers, in groups, and in movements to help relieve suffering?

11. For a closing, the group may benefit from a slow meditative, warm reading of the hymn, "O God, Our Help in Ages Past," p. 28 in *The Book of Hymns.*

Preparation for Session VI

Read Part II, Chapter 6 of the text. Read also the story of Jesus' experience in the Garden of Gethsemane and on the cross. Luke 22:39-54a, Luke 23:32-49. Read Isaiah 61:1-3, 10-11. Read Psalm 30:1-5 and Psalm 23. Read Revelation 21:1-6; 22:1-5.

Study Session VI

Assignments

Reading: Read again the Preface to the book, to review the author's purpose for study. Read Part II, Chapter 6 of the text. Read chapters 3 and 5 of Leslie Weatherhead's *The Will of God.*

Wall Displays: Display some of the art work and class members' responses to the other five sessions. This session could focus on signs and symbols that sustain us in our suffering: a chalice and loaf of bread; a towel and a basin; a baptismal bowl; a small pitcher of oil; pictures, paintings, sculpture of Christ on the Cross; pictures or paintings or banners of tongues of fire. Some pieces of art work or pictures depicting individuals or groups experiencing wholeness.

Worship Resources

Hymns: "The Lord Is My Shepherd," p. 961, "We Are One in the Spirit," p. 975, "Morning Has Broken," p. 929, *Supplement to the Book of Hymns;* "There Is a Balm in Gilead" (first stanza and chorus), p. 212, "God of Love and God of Power," p. 153, "Let Us Break Bread Together," p. 330, *The Book of Hymns;* "Leaning on the Everlasting Arms," p. 53, "Jesus, Savior, Pilot Me," p. 49, "Lift Every Voice and Sing," p. 210, *Songs of Zion*

Prayers and other Readings: "Every New Day I Have a New Chance," p. 140, "Choice," p. 141 of *Images: Women in Transition;* "Help Me to Say, 'Yes'," pages 120-123, Michel Quoist's *Prayers;* Isaiah 12:2-6; Luke 12:22-31 and Matthew 6:25-33; John 10:10b; I John 4:7-19. Prayer of John Baille in *A Guide to Prayer for Ministers and Other Servants,* by Rueben Job, p. 23.

Purpose

The purpose is to have a new/renewed experience of *shalom,* wholeness, peace; to gain a sense of one's worth and dignity and well-being; to share some special moments of healing and wholeness with one another in class.

Group Experience

1. In a Bible dictionary, look up and share the meaning of the two biblical words for peace, *shalom* and *eireine*. Ask the class to "brainstorm" for three minutes about all the possible meanings of *shalom* and put these on newsprint. Help the class to see that *shalom* is not a general, "out there" feeling, but is to be a personal sense of wholeness, harmony, and contentment.

2. Ask the class to share some situations of brokenness and wholeness in the world today. What are examples of individual and societal brokenness/wholeness? How can the church minister to individual brokenness? To societal brokenness?

3. What is the story that the Christian community has to tell? Why do we keep telling the story? How do we remember into the future?

4. The author writes that we "can connect into the power of the Spirit. . ." and quotes Julian of Norwich, who said that pain produced "a great oneing between Christ and us. . ." Ask the class to try to uncover some new meaning to describe what it is to "connect into the power of the Spirit" and to have a "oneing between Christ and us." How do we make it happen? Can we help this happen to another? How? What are some rituals we can use?

5. Do the exercise on picture-imagery suggested by the author. Have you ever use imagery to enable healing before? What experience have you had with this method?

6. The suggested "Closing Service of Worship" gives an excellent resource for ending the class's time together.

The Author

Robert T. Young is the senior minister of the Broad Street United Methodist Church, Statesville, NC. He has received an A.B. in religion from the University of North Carolina at Chapel Hill, a M.Div. from the Divinity School of Duke University, and a D.D. from Pfeiffer College, Misenheimer, NC.

Dr. Young is well known as a preacher, a teacher for Schools of Christian Mission, and a spiritual life retreat leader. He has written two books, *A Sprig of Hope*, published by Abingdon Press, and *Holy Moments*, published by The Upper Room.